THEODOR HERZL

If you will it, it is not a dream.

THEODOR HERZL

If you will it, it is not a dream.

This catalogue accompanies the
Yeshiva University Museum exhibition
Theodor Herzl: If you will it, it is not a dream,
April 6, 1997–July 31, 1998.
The exhibition and catalogue commemorate
the Centennial of the First Zionist Congress
and the
50th Anniversary of the establishment
of the State of Israel.

ISBN 0-945447-08-6

FOREWORD

In 1992, Manfred Anson first called us to suggest that we mark the 100th anniversary of the publication of *Der Judenstaat* with an exhibit of his Herzl collection. His idea was well-timed; we were anxious to explore the fascinating figure who galvanized world Jewry into creating a State. Although we had known Anson for years—he had lent pieces to both our Ashkenaz and Sepharad exhibitions—neither Bonni-Dara Michaels nor I was prepared for the torrent of Herzl-related artifacts that confronted us when we visited his home. To say we were amazed is an understatement.

Bonni-Dara was to repeat the trip more than a dozen times, sometimes alone, sometimes with other staff members or volunteers, as more and more "Herzliana" emerged from the nooks and crannies, the alcoves and closets and bookcases of Anson's modest home.

Manfred Anson, like many of us, belongs to the generation that grew up before the State of Israel came into being. In those days, Jewish children and their families, all over the world, belonged to Zionist groups, collected for the Jewish National Fund, sang the stirring songs of the movement, and watched—in countless darkened auditoriums—films like "Land of Promise" with commentary by Maurice Samuel (1935).

When Israel was declared a state in 1948, our rejoicing knew no bounds. The goals of Zionist striving had been accomplished. It was an experience and a sensation that most of us have never forgotten—the sweet smell of success, if you will.

Ted Comet of the Joint Distribution Committee has described how the Zionist dream in the years immediately after WWII was "a major force in uplifting the Jewish spirit. The idea of a land of one's own, where Jews could control their own destiny, countered the trauma of homelessness and helplessness.... With the establishment of the State...in one fell swoop, the Jews of Europe were suddenly transformed from victims to victors." Anson himself, a German born Jew who emigrated to Australia in 1940, was one of those victims.

Today, Zionism as a movement is at a crossroads. In the 100 years since Herzl's epiphany, "the Jewish world has become Zionized," to quote Rabbi Israel Miller, past president of the American Zionist Federation. While thousands of Diaspora Jews visit Israel annually, and Jewish students from almost every country in the world study there, the arduous, inspired, almost legendary struggle to achieve the Homeland is history.

In a museum, the material world of the past speaks to the generations of the present—interpreting, defining, and linking, transmitting messages across the generations. The Herzl exhibition gives us the opportunity to glimpse, learn, and make connections with a period of Jewish history those of us under the age of 50 have never known. Like the Exodus from Egypt, the events leading up to the creation of the State of Israel—events set in motion by a pamphlet—*Der Judenstaat*—are part of our collective history that all of us should know, and that should never be forgotten. As Herzl's contemporary, the Viennese author Stefan Zweig wrote:

> "Without realizing it, Herzl with his pamphlet had brought to flame
> the glowing coal of Judaism, long smouldering in the ashes, the
> thousand-year-old messianic dream, confirmed in the Holy Books,
> of the return to the Promised Land."

Sylvia Axelrod Herskowitz
August 1997

D9
151
H4
T364
1997
C.2

ACKNOWLEDGEMENTS

Many people deserve thanks for creating this exhibition and catalogue. Manfred Anson shared his vast collection and expertise and his infectious passion for Theodor Herzl's life and influence. Bonni-Dara Michaels, Museum Registrar/Curator, ably served as exhibition curator, assisted throughout the project by all members of YUM staff. A personal note of thanks to Professor Shlomo Eidelberg for his excellent, succinct biographical essay on Herzl, and to Professor Ruth Bevan for her thoughtful essay on Herzl as a nationalist leader. Gabriel Goldstein, YUM Curator, assisted with exhibition and catalogue planning, research and editing. Initial research and cataloguing of the Anson Collection was conducted with the help of Joelle Bollag, Assistant to the Director, and Rosette Pascal, Museum volunteer. Secretarial support was provided by Eleanor Chiger. The editing of this text involved the input of many individuals, including Randi Glickberg, YUM Deputy Director, and Yvonne Hudson, Yeshiva University Publications Department. Photography was provided by Norman Goldberg and Marc Becker, University Photographic Services Department. For the design of this publication, we are grateful to Judy Tucker, Art Director, University Graphics Department.

This exhibition was made possible through funding from the New York State Council on the Arts, with additional assistance provided by Mr. and Mrs. Marc Besen, Dr. Aaron J. Feingold and Brenda I. Liebowitz, and Daniel M. Friedenberg. All YUM exhibitions and programs are supported, in part, by the NYC Department of Cultural Affairs. For the publication of this catalogue, we are most grateful to Mary Smart and the Smart Family Foundation.

SAH

Table of Contents

BUSTS OF HERZL FROM THE EXHIBITION. TOP CENTER – CAT. NO. 157; UPPER RIGHT – CAT. NO. 156.

COMMEMORATIVE
TRIBUTE JOURNAL

Patron of
the Arts Dinner

YESHIVA UNIVERSITY MUSEUM

YESHIVA UNIVERSITY MUSEUM

Patron of the Arts Dinner

Commemorative Tribute Journal

produced for this special edition of the Herzl Catalogue

SEPTEMBER 22, 1997

THE PLAZA HOTEL • NEW YORK CITY

Ronnie Heyman, *Dinner Chairperson*

Earle Mack, *Honorary Chairperson*

Erica Jesselson, *Chairperson of Museum Board*

OMANUT AWARDEES

Andre Emmerich

Ben Meed

Yale Roe

Herman Shickman

Bruce Slovin

Judy Steinhardt

Vera Stern

Aaron Ziegelman

DINNER COMMITTEE

Stanley Batkin

Lore and Harry Bauer

Bob Becker

Dr. Jayne G. and Harvey Beker

Abby Belkin

Robert M. Beren

Ann and Kenneth Bialkin

Lotte and Ludwig Bravmann

Maureen Cogan

Mr. and Mrs. J. Morton Davidowitz (Davis)

Dr. Beatrice Friedland

Fanya Gottesfeld-Heller

Kathy Greenberg

Donald Hamburg

Karen and Elliot Hershberg

E. Billi Ivry

Ester Jesselson

Linda and Michael Jesselson

Doris and Dr. Ira Kukin

Lucy Lang

Tova Leidesdorf

Sivia and Jeffrey H. Loria

Ruth Mack

Wendy and Robert Meister

Ursula and Hermann Merkin

Ruth and Ted Mirvis

Dr. Alfred Moldovan

Gitta and Jack Nagel

Debby Neumark

A. Richard Parkoff

Jacob Reingold

Ingeborg and Ira L. Rennert

Pearl Resnick

Rose and Martin Romerovski

Rita Rosen

Belle Rosenbaum

Irving M. Rosenbaum

Romie Shapiro

Marianne and John Slade

Mary Smart

Rosa Strygler

Lynn and Sy Syms

Lucy Ullman

Putti Wimpfheimer

Barbara and Benjamin Zucker

Dr. Norman Lamm
President, Yeshiva University

With its mission to illuminate the wonders of our 3,000-year-old Jewish heritage, Yeshiva University Museum is more than a haven for priceless treasures of the Jewish past. A vibrant center of culture for the Jewish community, it is also a forum for learning that reaches beyond the University to touch the lives of both Jews and non-Jews, with exhibitions and educational programs that annually draw thousands to this gem "at the top of the city."

Exhibitions—such as "Sacred Realm: The Emergence of the Synagogue in the Ancient World," "The Kids Bridge," "Theodor Herzl: If You Will It, It Is Not A Dream," and "Ebrei Piemontesi: The Jews of Piedmont," and the work of living artists from Israel, the U.S., and around the world—convey the scope of history of the Jewish people to young and old alike and make our culture accessible for all to experience and enjoy.

Yeshiva University Museum owes a great debt of gratitude to the vision and generosity of its benefactors, Ludwig (of blessed memory) and Erica Jesselson, who have created and sustained this shining jewel. It is a true privilege to count them as respected leaders and cherished friends— not only of the Museum, but of the entire Yeshiva University family.

I extend my heartiest mazal tov to dinner chairperson Ronnie Heyman and honorary dinner chairperson Earle I. Mack, the members of the dinner committee, and the evening's eight distinguished honorees. May the Almighty bless you all, and may He guide you from strength to strength.

Ronnie Heyman
Dinner Chairperson

Earle Mack
Honorary Chairperson

The art historian Bernard Berenson said, "Art is not based on actuality, but on the wishes, dreams and aspirations of a people." Theodor Herzl, the subject of the catalogue in which this journal is enclosed, helped bring the dream of a people to reality.

Tonight we pay tribute to eight individuals—dedicated and visionary leaders in the world of art and culture—who have been instrumental in bringing artistic works to local, national, and international audiences. Through their endeavors, they have touched souls and enlightened and inspired minds.

Thank you for being with us this evening to salute their significant and enduring accomplishments. We are most grateful for your support of the Yeshiva University Museum, which is devoted to preserving and conveying the history of a people for the illumination of present and future generations.

Erica Jesselson

Chairperson, Yeshiva University Museum Board

We are gathered here tonight because we are committed to a high priority for the arts in Jewish life. From the biblical injunction to glorify the commandments up to the present-day cultural flowering of Jewish art in all its aspects, we as a people have been blessed with creative and inspired visionaries, artists and patrons.

Tonight we have singled out for recognition eight individuals who share our commitment to the arts: Andre Emmerich, Ben Meed, Yale Roe, Herman Shickman, Bruce Slovin, Judy Steinhardt, Vera Stern and Aaron Ziegelman. As artists, collectors, builders and shapers of Jewish arts institutions, they are possessed of uncommon vision, noble determination and exceptional taste. We applaud them all.

Sylvia A. Herskowitz

Director, Yeshiva University Museum

We are fortunate to live at a time when art is no longer the sheltered preserve of the elite. Especially in New York, with its panoply of art presenters, art creators, and art lovers, art seems to greet us at every turn of the road. But, with this largesse comes increased competition for funding, media coverage, and institutional support—a triad of concerns shared by every arts organization which only becomes more demanding as the organization grows.

YUM is now in its 24th year. Under the leadership of the Jesselson family, we are proud to have created a vibrant center for Jewish art in the midst of a great center of Jewish learning. Our exhibitions and catalogues are are known and acclaimed worldwide—the Herzl catalogue, which you are holding in your hands, being our 21st and latest offering.

Our future, quite literally, is also in your hands. The enthusiastic encouragement and generosity of our benefactors have enabled us to come this far. We trust that your continued felicitous support will inspire our continued growth and success.

Andre Emmerich

Andre Emmerich was born in Frankfurt, Germany, raised in Amsterdam, Holland, and emigrated to the United States in 1940. In 1954, he founded the Andre Emmerich Gallery, which specializes in pre-Columbian and classical art and antiquities and contemporary American and European art. The roster of artists represented reads like a Who's Who in modern art: Albers, Avery, Hoffmann, Haring, Hockney, Lieberman, Caro, Olitski, and others.

Mr. Emmerich is the author of two books, "Art Before Columbus," and "Sweat of the Sun and Tears of the Moon: Gold and Silver in Pre-Columbian Art," as well as numerous scholarly articles. He has taught at the Salzburg Seminar in America Studies in Austria and the New School for Social Research in New York and lectured extensively at museums and universities throughout the U.S.

He is a member of the board of the National Association of Dealers in Ancient, Oriental and Primitive Art, past president of the Art Dealers Association of America, and serves on the Storm King Art Center Regional Advisory Committee and the visiting committee of the Allen Memorial Art Museum at Oberlin College, his alma mater.

Benjamin Meed

Benjamin Meed was born in Warsaw, survived World War II by working as a slave laborer for the Germans, survived 1000 days in the Warsaw Ghetto, and was a member with his wife, Vladka, of the Warsaw underground. When they came to America in 1946, the Meeds chose to put their efforts into the founding of the American Gathering of Jewish Holocaust Survivors, now numbering 100,000 survivors and their families. Mr. Meed has been president of that organization since 1981, as well as president of the Warsaw Ghetto Resistance Organization and a member of the U.S. Holocaust Memorial Council and chairman of its Museum Content Committee. He has also served for the past 34 years as chairman of the annual Yom Hashoah Commemoration in New York.

It was Ben Meed who introduced President Clinton at the special White House reception marking the opening of the U.S. Holocaust Museum in Washington, D.C. Every day of his life is spent working to keep the memory of the Holocaust alive, so that it will never happen again. His commitment now is to create a permanent record of all Holocaust survivors and their children through the national registry of the American Gathering. This registry of 100,000 files on Holocaust survivors and their families is permanently housed at the U.S. Holocaust Museum.

Yale Roe

Yale Roe is an amazing amalgam of creativity and Jewish commitment. After a 15 year management career with ABC-TV, the building of a TV station in Chicago, and the authorship of two books, one of which is now a university textbook in broadcasting, Mr. Roe moved to Jerusalem. There, he created TV documentaries seen throughout the world and which earned numerous awards.

Today, Yale Roe is an independent filmmaker with offices in New York and Jerusalem. His television documentaries of special Jewish events, have been commissioned by UJA, Israel Bonds, and the Yeshiva University Museum. Later this year, he will release a TV special, "Jerusalem: The City Touched by God," hosted by Liv Ullmann.

Working with Yale Roe is a satisfying and happy experience. His genuine love of Israel and of Jews everywhere has shaped his life and career, and endowed him with the gentle, caring personality which endears him to everyone.

Herman Shickman

Herman Shickman is owner of the H. Shickman Gallery, which specializes in the sale of Old Master paintings. One of the Gallery's major purchases was Titian's "Venus and Adonis" on behalf of the J. Paul Getty Museum in Malibu, California. In 1991, he and his wife, Lila, donated a painting by 17th century Flemish painter Frans Synders to the National Gallery of Art in Washington, D.C.

Mr. Shickman is a founder of the Israel Museum and the Carlebach Institute at Israel's Bar-Ilan University, as well as an active supporter of numerous Jewish causes, including Shaare Zedek Hospital in Jerusalem.

Born in Hamburg, Germany, he came to the United States in 1938 and served as a captain in the U.S. Army.

Bruce Slovin

Bruce Slovin has reached the heights of the business world as president and a director of MacAndrews & Forbes Holdings, Inc. and Revlon Group Incorporated, its subsidiary. But we honor him tonight for the vision and energy with which he has led the YIVO Institute for Jewish Research.

As Chairman of the Board of YIVO, Mr. Slovin envisioned a long-range plan that astounded the Jewish world with its boldness—the creation of a consortium of research, archival and exhibiting institutions that together would form a Center for Jewish History. At a time of increasing fragmentation and divisiveness, his plan offers a striking and original modus operandi: the sharing of technology, resources and space in pursuit of a common goal—the collection, preservation, and interpretation of the Jewish experience.

Mr. Slovin holds leadership positions in numerous other communal, civic and arts organizations, including the American Jewish Historical Society and the Educational Alliance.

Judy Steinhardt

Judy Steinhardt has been a devoted leader of the American Friends of the Israel Museum since 1978 and its president since 1995. She has also served numerous other arts institutions and currently is a member of the boards of the Institute of Fine Arts, Brooklyn Botanic Garden, and Caramoor, and various committees of the Metropolitan Museum of Art.

Mrs. Steinhardt is a graduate of the University of Michigan and Tufts University School of Education. Her enthusiasm, engaging personality, and creative imagination are innate talents she brings to every project she undertakes—which is why she has become a sought after leader in the Jewish world at large and in the art world in particular.

Vera Stern

The America-Israel Cultural Foundation is the focus of Vera Stern's volunteer efforts. AICF's Sharett Scholarship program, which awards over 600 scholarships and fellowships each year, has such famous alumni as Itzhak Perlman, Pinchas Zukerman, Gil Shaham, Menashe Kadishman and others. For 40 years, Mrs. Stern has devoted her efforts to AICF, and for the past five years she has been its president.

The effort to save Carnegie Hall in 1960 was greatly assisted by Mrs. Stern, who continues to serve on its special events committee. With her incredible experience in the musical world, she has organized many benefit events for the causes in which she believes and reached out to touch the lives of countless Jews in Israel and throughout the world.

Aaron Ziegelman

Aaron Ziegelman lost his father at the age of six, on the eve of the Holocaust. When he emigrated to America in 1938 with his mother and sister, he was unaware that he would ever see his other relatives again. Four years after they left their village of Luboml, the Nazi forces wiped out the entire community.

Mr. Ziegelman did not find out that any of his relatives survived until 1991, when he met a man by the same name and learned that there were indeed other relatives alive. This chance meeting spurred him to begin searching for his roots. Since he had built a very successful career in real estate, Mr. Ziegelman was able to totally commit himself to the search—with all his heart, his soul, and his resources. The project took three years, during which time Mr. Ziegelman hired a curator/researcher, and traveled all over the world to locate Luboml survivors, videotape them, and collect their memories and memorabilia.

The Luboml Exhibition Project, the culmination of Mr. Ziegelman's quest, restores his beloved Jewish community to a living memory. It is his gift to his family, to those who perished and those who survived, and to present and future generations.

IN HONOR OF

ERICA JESSELSON

AND IN FOND MEMORY OF

LUDWIG JESSELSON

LOTTE AND LUDWIG BRAVMANN

IN HONOR OF MOM

AND HER DEDICATION TO

JEWISH CULTURE

AND ART

THE JESSELSON FAMILY

CONGRATULATIONS

TO ALL THE WORTHY

HONOREES

INGEBORG AND IRA LEON RENNERT

CONGRATULATIONS TO

ALL THE STALWARTS

OF THE YESHIVA UNIVERSITY MUSEUM

AND TO THEIR BRIGHT NEW FUTURE

THE SLOVIN FAMILY

CENTER FOR JEWISH HISTORY

IN TRIBUTE TO

ERICA JESSELSON

FOR ALL SHE HAS DONE TO

PERPETUATE THE AESTHETIC SIDE

OF OUR JEWISH TRADITIONS

THE HEYMAN FAMILY

TO A GREAT TEAM

ERICA JESSELSON

AND

SYLVIA HERSKOWITZ

AND ALL WHO WORK WITH THEM SO WELL.

OVER VERY BEST WISHES ON

YOUR FUTURE MOVE!

ANN AND MARCUS ROSENBERG

IN HONOR OF

ERICA JESSELSON

FOR ALL OF HER HARD WORK

IN MAKING THE YESHIVA UNIVERSITY MUSEUM

A SUCCESS

JUDY AND MICHAEL STEINHARDT

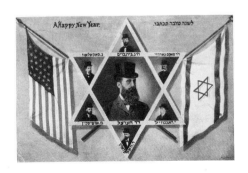

CONGRATULATIONS TO

THE HONOREES

FROM

FANYA GOTTESFELD-HELLER

BENJAMIN HELLER

BEST WISHES

THE MACK FAMILY

LYNN AND SY SYMS

Proudly
Join

YESHIVA UNIVERSITY
MUSEUM

In Honoring

ERICA JESSELSON

IN TRIBUTE TO

ERICA JESSELSON

AND THE

JESSELSON FAMILY

WHO ARE THE GUIDING LIGHTS OF

THIS IMPORTANT MUSEUM

MR. AND MRS. GEORGE KLEIN

BEST WISHES TO THE PATRONS OF THE ARTS

ANDRE EMMERICH

BEN MEED

YALE ROE

HERMAN SHICKMAN

BRUCE SLOVIN

JUDY STEINHARDT

VERA STERN

AARON ZIEGELMAN

FROM

HARVEY AND JAYNE BEKER

BEST WISHES

MAUREEN AND MARSHALL COGAN

TRACE INTERNATIONAL HOLDING, INC.
FOUNDATION

TO

ERICA JESSELSON

MAY YOU GO FROM STRENGTH TO STRENGTH

FOR MANY MORE SUCCESSFUL DINNERS

CHARLES DIMSTON

WE HONOR

ERICA JESSELSON

FOR HER MANY EFFORTS

AND WONDERFUL LEADERSHIP

IN SUPPORT OF THE

YESHIVA UNIVERSITY MUSEUM,

A NEW YORK LANDMARK INSTITUTION

LEO AND JULIA FORCHHEIMER FOUNDATION

IN HONOR OF

ERICA JESSELSON

A GREAT LADY AND THE DRIVING FORCE OF

YESHIVA UNIVERSITY MUSEUM.

TO HER GOOD HEALTH

DE. BEATRICE L. FRIEDLAND

IN HONOR OF

ERICA JESSELSON

AND

JUDY STEINHARDT

HARRY AND MATTA FREUND

JAY AND DIANE GOLDSMITH

IN HONOR OF

ERICA JESSELSON

AN ADMIRED FRIEND AND INSPIRED LEADER

MIRIAM AND ALAN GOLDBERG

OUR CONGRATULATIONS

AND ADMIRATION TO THIS YEAR'S

DISTINGUISHED HONOREES

AND TO

ERICA JESSELSON

FOR HER EXEMPLARY LEADERSHIP

RUTH AND DAVID GOTTESMAN

CONGRATULATIONS

TO ALL

GUESTS OF HONOR

AND TO

MRS. J

WHO HONORS ALL HER GUESTS

.

RUTH AND TED MIRVIS

THE PARKOFF FAMILY

DEBRA, RICHARD, SAMARA TOVAH

AND ADAM LAWRENCE

CONGRATULATIONS TO THE

YESHIVA UNIVERSITY MUSEUM

AND EVERY GOOD WISH FOR THE FUTURE

MORTY AND ENIA PROPP

IN HONOR OF OUR GOOD FRIENDS

ERICA

AND

LUCY

PUTTI AND ERNST

CONGRATULATIONS TO

ERICA JESSELSON

FOR HER GREAT LEADERSHIP

AND FOR THE

WONDERFUL SELECTION OF HONOREES

JUDY AND BURT RESNICK

FOR

ERICA JESSELSON

AN INCREDIBLE WOMAN

רפואה שלמה

ANITA AND YALE ROE

IN HONOR OF OUR GOOD FRIENDS

YALE ROE

AND

JUDY STEINHARDT

JOAN AND ALAN SAFIR

WE APPLAUD

BRUCE SLOVIN

AND

ALL THE RECIPIENTS

ON THE OMANUT AWARD

S THE HEMANO GROUP

SOLVING INVESTMENT CHALLENGES
WITH WISDOM EXPERIENCE

SAN FRANCISCO

SOTHEBY'S

CONGRATULATES

ANDRE EMMERICH

AND IS PLEASED

TO SUPPORT

YESHIVA UNIVERSITY

MUSEUM

SOTHEBY'S

WITH LOVE AND ADMIRATION TO

ERICA JESSELSON

LOVE,

ROSA STRYGLER

Aaron Ziegelman and
the Luboml Exhibition Project
are pleased to be collaborating with
Yeshiva University Museum
on the New York presentation
of our exhibition.

REMEMBERING

Luboml

Images of a Jewish Community

The Gallery
Benjamin N. Cardozo School of Law
55 Fifth Ave. at 12th St.

The exhibit will be on view
September 9 - December 31, 1997

CONGRATULATIONS

TO ALL THE HONOREES

ON THIS WELL DESERVED HONOR

DIANE BELFER

IN TRIBUTE TO

ERICA JESSELSON

WHOSE ART OF DEVOTION TO THE JEWISH PEOPLE EVERYWHERE

IS FURTHER ENHANCED BY HER DEVOTION TO THE ARTS AND

THE YESHIVA UNIVERSITY MUSEUM, HER CREATION

NERI BLOOMFIELD

IN HONOR AND RESPECT

FOR

ERICA JESSELSON

GITI AND JACK BENDHEIM AND FAMILY

IN TRIBUTE TO A GRAND LADY

ERICA JESSELSON

WHOSE CREATIVE LEADERSHIP ON BEHALF OF THE YESHIVA

UNIVERSITY MUSEUM AND ALL OUR AFFILIATES SCHOOLS

OF YESHIVA UNIVERSITY IS AN INSPIRATION TO US.

MAZAL TOV GREETINGS TO

ALL THE HONOREES

SHEPSIE AND JUDAH FEINERMAN

IN HONOR OF

ERICA

WHOSE DEDICATED LEADERSHIP HAS ENRICHED

JEWISH ART AND CULTURE

AND CONGRATULATIONS TO THE

OUTSTANDING HONOREES

MR. AND MRS. MORITZ GOLDFEIER

IN HONOR OF OUR FRIEND

ERICA JESSELSON

ERWIN HERLING AND TOVA LEIDESDORF

IN HONOR OF

ERICA JESSELSON

FOR HER STEADFAST, OUTSTANDING

AND DEDICATED DEVOTION TO THE

YESHIVA UNIVERSITY MUSEUM

E. BILLI IVRY

IN HONOR OF

ERICA JESSELSON

MICKI AND GARY JOSEPH

BEST WISHES

IRA AND DORIS KUKIN

TO

ERICA

WITH LOVE

LUCY AND FAMILY

THE NASH FAMILY FOUNDATION

WITH LOVE AND ADMIRATION

FOR

ERICA JESSELSON

PEARL RESNICK

IN HONOR OF

ERICA JESSELSON

LORE AND HARRY BAUER

One day, Honi was walking on the road and saw a man planting a carob tree.

Puzzled, Honi asked, "How long does it take for this tree to bear fruit?"

The man replied: "Seventy years."

Honi asked again, "And do you believe you will be alive in another seventy years?"

The man replied: "When I came into this world, there were carob trees with fruit ripe for picking. Just as my parents planted for me, so will I plant for my children."

Talmud Ta'anit 23a

Charles and Lynn Schusterman
Family Foundation

IN HONOR OF

ERICA J.

ROBERT
PAYNE
FURS

ANITA AND ROBERT PAYNE

CONGRATULATIONS TO

ALL THE HONOREES

DR. BELLE ROSENBAUM

CONGRATULATIONS

TO ALL THE

HONOREES

BLANCHE AND ROMIE SHAPIRO

TO

ERICA

MAZAL TOV ON YOUR CONTINUED SUCCESS

JOHN AND MARIANNE SLADE

IN HONOR OF

OUR FRIENDS

ERICA JESSELSON

AND

AARON ZIEGELMAN

CLAIRE AND ALBERT SCHUSSLER

THE STAFF OF THE YESHIVA UNIVERSITY MUSEUM,
WITH WARMEST AFFECTION, CONGRATULATES THE
1997 PATRONS OF THE ARTS
AND THANKS THE JESSELSON FAMILY
FOR THEIR LEADERSHIP AND INSPIRED VISION

SYLVIA A. HERSKOWITZ, Director
RANDI GLICKBERG, Deputy Director
RACHELLE BRADT, Curator of Education
ELEANOR CHIGER, Office Manager
ELIZABETH DIAMENT, Assistant Curator of Education
GABRIEL GOLDSTEIN, Curator of Judaica
BONNI-DARA MICHAELS, Museum Registrar/Curator
JUDITH WOLF, Assistant Curator of Education
REBA WULKAN, Contemporary Exhibitions Coordinator

FOR THE

YESHIVA UNIVERSITY MUSEUM

WITH OUR THANKS FOR PROVIDING US

WITH OPPORTUNITIES TO LEARN AND TO TEACH –

לבנות ולהבנות

THE DOCENTS OF YESHIVA UNIVERSITY MUSEUM

WE REGRET THE OMISSION

OF ANY CONGRATULATORY MESSAGES

RECEIVED SUBSEQUENT TO THE

PUBLICATION OF THIS JOURNAL

FRIENDS

MR. LAWRENCE I. ATLAS
in honor of Mrs. Erica Jesselson

MR. AND MRS. LOUIS BARNETT
in honor of Mrs. Erica Jesselson

MR. AND MRS. JACK A. BELZ

MR. AND MRS. IRWIN CHANALES

MR. AND MRS. C. DANIEL CHILL

MR. BERNARD CIMBERBERG
in honor of Mr. Aaron Ziegelman

MR. AND MRS. LEON EISENBERG

MR. AND MRS. ROBERT FISCHER

MR. AND MRS. JOSEPH H. FLOM

MR. AND MRS. MORRIS L. GREEN

MR. AND MRS. HARRY GROSS

MRS. HELEN GROSS

CAROLA S. GRUEN
in honor of Erica Jesselson

RABBI WILLIAM AND SYLVIA HERSKOWITZ
in honor of Erica Jesselson

MR. AND MRS. MARTIN KIMMEL

MR. AND MRS. FRED LONNER

MRS. EDITH LUSTIG

MR. AND MRS. MICHAEL MARTON

MR. AND MRS. MOSES MARX

MR. AND MRS. EDWARD H. MERRIN

MR. AND MRS. EDGAR J. NATHAN, 3RD

FRIENDS

MR. AND MRS. HOWARD ROSEN

MS. RITA ROSEN

MR. IRVING ROSENBAUM

MR. HENRY ROTHSCHILD
in honor of Mrs. Jesselson

CHAROLTTE SCHNEIERSON

MR. AND MRS. ROBERT SCHWALBE
in tribute to Erica Jesselson

MR. AND MRS. JERRY SIEGELMAN
in honor of Mr. Aaron Ziegelman

JEANETTE R. SOLOMON
in honor of Judy Steinhardt and Vera Stern

JOSEPH AND DIANE STEINBERG

MRS. LEE DYM WEINBACH
in honor of Erica Jesselson

MR. AND MRS. HARVEY WOLINETZ

Why I Collected Herzl

When the Nazis came to power in 1933, I was eleven years old. Three years later, in 1936, I was thrown out of my Reali School in order to make it Judenrein. So, at age 14 my parents enrolled me in the only Jewish Horticultural College in Germany, near Hanover in the north, over a day's journey by rail. It was there that I had my first contact with Zionism by joining Habonim, a group run by the older boys, whose aim was for us to go to Palestine upon graduation. We all learned the old popular Hebrew songs of that period, sang them at our *Sichas*, and I was given a small booklet to read by a man named Theodor Herzl: *Der Judenstaat*. At that age I barely comprehended it, read perhaps a small part of it and gave it back. A Jewish State was a dream while the clouds of war were already rolling above our heads.

Then came my lucky immigration to England and from there to Australia in 1940. WWII began while I was working on a farm and eventually I joined the army and was discharged in 1946 to begin another life. While I was busy trying to make a living, Herzl was far from my mind. But, once again, a friend and I went to Zionist meetings as Israel began to evolve into the state I had read about 14 years before. While collecting money for the J.N.F. at street corners and functions I wasn't aware of Herzl's prophecy that in 50 years there would be a Jewish State and he was only wrong by one year—1897 to 1948.

In 1961 I won a raffle trip to Israel. It was a long way from Australia but at last I entered the Jewish State that was only 13 years old. At long last I stood at Herzl's grave which was still covered with the red soil of the highest hill in the new city, a few flowers covering the earth. Standing there alone, only the wind heard my Kaddish for our great leader.

Another immigration followed—I came to the United States in 1963. While walking the avenues and streets of New York, starting all over again, I came upon the Jewish Museum and found a small room, quite hidden away from all the other treasures, filled with medals of Jewish people and institutions as well as ancient Jewish coins. On that day Numismatics became my hobby. I learned that there were two men who had more medals made for them than anyone else: Sir Moses Montefiore and Theodor Herzl. This is how my thirty year involvement with Herzl began. One medal followed another, one plaque followed another, until one room of our house was completely covered with them.

The Judenstaat now being a reality I reread the book to the end, this time in English. Soon after, I was able to buy the original booklet in German, signed by Herzl! With this a whole new horizon opened. Why only collect medals and other metallic objects such as busts, plates and plaques when so much more was available?

Eventually everything comes to New York, and the city became my treasure house where I continually hunted for Herzl memorabilia. It was quite obvious that I needed all the books he wrote, his daily journals, his speeches to the various congresses, his letters asking for money for the cause, and invitations to the First Zionist Congress in Basel in 1897.

Naturally, I also needed all the Herzl postcards printed in every country in Europe. With the help of postcard dealers called Deltiologists I found those elusive pieces of paper in every color and in combination with other Zionist leaders. From postcards followed, naturally, stamps. How could I have ignored Herzl stamps? I had to invade another hobby, Philatelics, which produced entirely different images of Herzl on even smaller pieces of paper. On this theme, Israel's Postal Department was outdone by the Jewish National Fund which had produced Herzl stamps called tabs since its inception early in this century by Professor Shapira and Dr. Bodenheimer. How could I not have known about them earlier? A new hunt developed to find Herzl stamps in every color and printed in different countries.

While reading Herzl's diaries I learned that everything began with the Dreyfus Trials in Paris. Of course, I needed a few mementos of this infamous affair: satirical postcards, anti-semitic posters and again medals—all had to be found and added to my overflowing boxes.

Still another vista opened to me when it was brought to my attention that great men, particularly good looking ones, are painted by contemporary artists as well as later ones. Originals were out of the question of course, those by painters such as Struck, Pilichowski, Lilien or Patai. Only prints and etchings could be found.

One of the great admirers of Herzl was the artist Boris Schatz who established the Bezalel Art School during the first decade of this century. He knew Herzl and his school produced many images of him in every medium. Some of the finest portraits of Herzl were created by the pupils of the school: Samuel Kretschmer, Murro and Schatz himself. Naturally, I had to acquire some of those, and at last I found the most famous plaque by Kretschmer which was reproduced over and over again in smaller versions by numerous organizations.

Eventually it became necessary for me to begin collecting memorabilia of Herzl's greatest achievement—the organization of the Zionist Congresses, of which the first was held in Basel one hundred years ago. This meant that a quite separate collection had to be started. Every Congress produced commemorative postcards commissioned from important artists of that time. Those cards are perhaps the most elusive and expensive pieces of paper a collector can look for. To get them all is almost impossible and only at great expense. At least I tried.

As a collector, sooner or later, one has to make the acquaintance of dealers who often find things one desperately needs. But there are also people who handle estates that often include things that have been put away for many years. One day an attorney called to ask if I was interested in a copy of Herzl's wills. In an hour I was at his office in midtown NY where I bought three copies of three different wills. Herzl changed his will several times—one of them stated his wish to be buried in the Jewish State.

To sum up, I have been fortunate to enjoy the indulgence of my wife and children who may have had to go without a few things important to them because Herzl was so important to me. The romance of collecting Herzl over the past 30 years has been one of the more rewarding things I have done for myself, my family, and, hopefully, for the Zionist cause.

Manfred Anson
March 1997

Theodor Herzl: From Vision to Reality

Shlomo Eidelberg

Zionism Prior to Herzl

Hess, Pinsker and the Hovevei Zion

The history of the modern Zionist movement began early in the nineteenth century. The movement spread faster in Eastern Europe, than in Western Europe and America, due to the combination of anti-semitism and economic problems. While most of the Zionist leaders came from Western Europe, one of the Zionist movement's early champions was Moses Hess, a Jewish philosopher and writer who lived in Cologne. In 1840, he wrote: "We will always be strangers among nations who grant us rights from humanitarian or legal motives but will not respect us so long as we relegate our greatest Jewish traditions to a secondary place…" In his book, *Rome and Jerusalem* (1862), Hess discusses the rebirth of the Jewish nation through colonization in Palestine. His views forecasted future events and his work influenced many, including Leon Pinsker and Theodor Herzl.

Leon Pinsker was a Russian Jew educated in Western Europe. A physician and son of Simcha Pinsker, a famous Hebraist with a worldly education—Leon became concerned with the Jewish situation after the Russian pogroms in 1881. In his seminal work, *Auto-Emancipation*, (1882) he argued that anti-semitism was not a transient problem, but a disease. To overcome it he recommended the Jews must form a nation with their own culture. Eventually Pinsker joined the Hovevei Zion, a movement whose goal was the colonization of Palestine. During the 1884 Congress of Hovevei Zion at Kattowitz, he was elected President and served in that position until his death in 1891. Ultimately, the Hovevei Zion were absorbed into the new movement of Herzlian Zionism.

Curiously, Herzl had not heard of either Pinsker or Hess's work until he became deeply involved in the Zionist movement. After reading Pinsker's pamphlet, Herzl wrote in 1896, that he might never have written *Der Judenstaat (The Jewish State)* if he had known about *Auto-Emancipation*.

Herzl

His Life Until 1895

Theodor Herzl was born on May 2, 1860, in Budapest. His parents, Jacob and Jeanette, both came from upper-middle class backgrounds. His father was a banker; his mother's family owned a successful clothing business. Although Herzl's parents were not observant Jews, they kept certain traditions; Herzl's early childhood did not lack a religious foundation. He attended a synagogue with his father every Sabbath, and at the age of eight, his father enrolled him as a member of the *Hevra Kadisha*, the community burial society, under his Hebrew name, Benyamin Zeev ben Yakov Herzl.

There is a story that Herzl's ancestors escaped to Turkey during the expulsion of the Jews from Spain in 1492, and later moved to Semlin, at that time part of the Turkish Empire. Theodor's paternal grandfather, Simon Leib Herzl, who was active in the Jewish congregation in Semlin, is believed to have been a follower of Haham Judah ben Solomon Hai Alkalai (1792–1878), a Sephardic rabbi in the community of Semlin and an early Zionist. Simon Leib came to Budapest in 1873 to attend his grandson's bar-mitzvah, a grand occasion for Herzl's entire family. Theodor, who had practiced diligently, was called to read a portion of the Torah. He never forgot this milestone which may have planted the seeds for his later Zionist beliefs. However, Herzl later became increasingly influenced by his mother's love for German culture and literature, and from the age of sixteen through eighteen took part in the German Self-Education Society at a Budapest liberal arts high school.

In 1878, after the death of their only daughter Pauline from tuberculosis, the Herzl family moved to Vienna where Theodor attended law school at the University. In the 1880's numerous anti-liberal German and Austrian organizations initiated a wave of conservatism and anti-semitism that swept through Austria. Herzl, who by then considered himself an Austrian patriot, was deeply agitated by the violence. He became actively involved in the liberal student Cultural Association, where he faithfully attended discussions and directed its literary evenings.

Although he no longer attended synagogue as he had in his youth, he was still very concerned with the Jewish question. After reading Eugen Dühring's anti-semitic book, *The Jewish Problem as a Problem of Race, Morals and Culture*, Herzl wrote the following in his diary:

> *If Dühring, who unites so much undeniable intelligence with so much universality of knowledge, can write like this, what are we to expect from the ignorant masses.*

Herzl's feeling about Dühring's were only part of his anxiety about the Jewish plight. The anti-semitism that Dühring's work represented was seeping into University life. When Herzl learned that his fencing fraternity, where he was an active member, had joined in an anti-semitic demonstration, he promptly resigned.

In 1884, Herzl obtained his law degree, for a time, aspiring to become a judge. Fully aware of the powerful Viennese bureaucracy and the its prevailing prejudice against Jews, he realized he had little chance of fulfilling his career goal. In 1885, after only one year as a practicing lawyer, he decided to give up law and become a journalist and playwright. Herzl became involved with the Viennese cultural elite, many of whom were Jews; among his acquaintances were writers Arthur Schnitzler and Stefan Zweig, composer Gustav Mahler, and Dr. Sigmund Freud, who later broke with Herzl following his involvement with Zionism. (Of these famous figures, Zweig was the only one who remembered Herzl kindly in his book *The World of Yesterday*.) Herzl contributed regularly to various well-known newspapers, reporting mainly on his impressions and observations on various European cities. In 1892 his success seemed boundless. While plays were being performed in leading theaters in Vienna, he was appointed to the staff of the *Neue Freie Presse*, one of Western Europe's most prominent newspapers and wrote the popular feuilleton that was enjoyed by its readers.

1894–1895

Theodor Herzl's life took a dramatic turn when Captain Alfred Dreyfus was found guilty of military espionage in France in October 1894. The verdict left the country in an uproar, for Dreyus had steadfastly maintained his innocence throughout his trial. Many questioned the verdict. Even when Dreyfus was publicly degraded in the courtyard of the École Militaire in 1895, he never admitted his guilt. As a journalist, Theodor Herzl attended the entire trial; his consciousness was permanently altered by the case. Confident of Dreyfus' innocence, Herzl wrote in his diary:

> *The Dreyfus case embodies more than a judicial error; it embodies*
> *the desire of the vast majority of the French to condemn a Jew, and*
> *to condemn all Jews in this one Jew… in republican, modern, civi-*
> *lized France, a hundred years after the Declaration of the Rights of*
> *Man. The French people, or at any rate the greater part of the*
> *French people, does not want to extend the rights of man to Jews…*

The anti-semitism unleashed by the Dreyfus case was the fire that ignited Herzl's soul. *The New Ghetto*, written between October 1 – November 8, 1894, was Herzl's first play dealing with Jews. In many respects, the plot parallels Herzl's own life. The transformation in the main character, lawyer Jacob Samuel, mirrored Herzl's own change of heart. *The New Ghetto* stresses that even the most assimilated Jews inhabit an invisible ghetto in a gentile world—an issue that clearly echoed Herzl's own situation.

Now, Herzl began to act on the ideas he had written about—he yearned to create a homeland for the Jewish people. In June 1895, Herzl submitted a plan to Baron Maurice de Hirsch, a wealthy Jewish philanthropist, concerning possible political action for the nascent Zionist movement. This was the first time that Herzl discussed his ideas on the Jewish dilemma with an outsider. But Baron Hirsch—more concerned with settling Jews in colonies in Argentina and helping poor Jews in Europe—denied Herzl's request for aid. However, Herzl was not deterred.

November 1895–August 1897

Herzl decided to thoroughly explain his idea of a Jewish homeland in order to reach Jewry at large. On November 21, 1895, he went to England on the advice of his colleague Max Nordau, a physician and writer and an early follower of political Zionism. Nordau believed that England was an important political contact for Herzl. There, Herzl met the English novelist and poet Israel Zangwill, as well as other influential Jews who shared his dream of Palestine as a Jewish homeland. Zangwill introduced Herzl to Colonel Albert Goldsmid, a soldier by profession, born to parents who had converted to Christianity. When Goldsmid shared how he returned to Judaism as an adult and his strong Zionist convictions, Herzl recognized a kindred spirit.

Herzl returned to Vienna inspired. He decided to revise his sixty-five page pamphlet on the Jewish homeland that he had written earlier that year. The result was *Der Judenstaat—The Jewish State*, published on February 14, 1896. This book describes Herzl's own philosophy of the world, and his thoughts on the condition of the Jewish state, as well as his ideas of science and technology. His ideas are best presented in his own words:

> *The distinctive nationality of the Jews neither can, will, nor must be destroyed. It cannot be destroyed because external enemies consolidate it. It will not be destroyed: this it has shown during 2,000 years of appalling suffering. It must be not destroyed...attempts at colonization made even by really benevolent men, interesting attempts though they were, have so far been unsuccessful. These attempts were interesting, in that they represented on a small scale the practical forerunners of the idea of a Jewish State. They have, of course, done harm also. The transportation of anti-semitism to new districts, which is the inevitable consequence of such artificial infiltration, seems to be the least of these evils...Let the sovereignty be granted us over a portion of the globe large enough to satisfy the reasonable requirements of a nation; the rest we shall manage ourselves.*

Continuing, Herzl gave a detailed outline as to how the Jewish state should develop.

Der Judenstaat was translated into several languages and quickly gained the attention of Jews everywhere. Herzl sent copies of the book to a number of non-Jewish statesmen, including English prime minister William Gladstone. The reaction of the public was varied. Although *The Jewish State* made a great impression on many, some did not view the work favorably. In general, Western European Jews were less supportive of a Jewish homeland than Eastern European Jews. There was less sympathy towards a politically recognized Jewish homeland in areas where Jews were more satisfied with their government.

Despite many disappointments Herzl continued with his crusade. During 1896, Herzl attempted to obtain political endorsements for his idea of a Jewish homeland. On March 10, he met with the Reverend William H. Hechler, chaplain of the British Embassy to Vienna. Hechler promised to assist in obtaining an audience for Herzl with the Grand Duke of Baden and the Duke's nephew, the German Emperor, to discuss possible German support of a Jewish nation. On April 23, in Karlsruhe, Herzl met with the Grand Duke who reacted positively to his plan for a Jewish homeland. Two months later, Herzl met the Grand Vizier, the prime minister of the

Turkish Empire, to which Palestine belonged. Although Herzl left Constantinople a week later without any definitive support from the government, he was awarded the distinguished Order of Medjidje, third class.

When, in July 1896, Herzl met Baron Edmond de Rothschild in Paris, he hoped to find the Baron sympathetic to his cause. Rothschild, who had already sponsored several unprofitable Jewish philanthropic colonies in Palestine, seemed a likely source for aid. To Herzl's dismay, the Baron refused to help because he disagreed with Herzl's plans for political Zionism and the creation of a Jewish state.

Next, Herzl decided to air his ideas before Jewish representatives from throughout the world. On March 6, 1897, the Actions Committee of the Zionist organization decided on a Congress to be held in Munich on August 25. But the Jewish community of Munich protested openly against political Zionism and Herzl's ideas. So the Congress was moved to Basel, along with the controversy.

In July 1897, both the Federation of Orthodox Rabbis and the Federation of Liberal Rabbis issued statements against the Congress, emphasizing that Zionism contradicts the "prophetic message of Jewry and the duty of every Jew to belong without reservation to the fatherland in which he lives." To rebuke these claims, Herzl announced that several influential East European Rabbis supported Political Zionism. Herzl and his followers published the first issue of *Die Welt* in Cologne on June 4, 1897. This paper became the voice of the First Zionist Congress.

The First Congress
Basel, August 29–31, 1897

The First Zionist Congress was a landmark, not only in Zionist history, but in Jewish history. It was the most irrefutable evidence of the existence of a Jewish nation: it drew Jews from all lands and cultures, religious Jews and freethinkers, Jews from every station of life and belonging to all classes. The Congress gradually became the Parliament of a homeless nation.

In his speech before the Congress Herzl discussed the main problem facing Zionism—turning ideology into concrete action. Herzl's first step was to mobilize the Jewish people to create a nation on a strong foundation that was, "...a return to Judaism before the return of the Jewish land," suggesting the desire of the Jews to return to their Homeland and create a unified Jewish culture. There were also numerous addresses about the condition of Jews throughout the world—Russia, Austria, Galicia, Bukovina, Roumania, Germany, Hungary, Great Britain and America.

One of the important decisions was the designation of the shekel as the fee for each individual membership in the Zionist organization. This continued until the establishment of the State of Israel.

Issues concerning the colonization of Palestine and the question of Jewish national culture, particularly the cultivation of the Hebrew language, were discussed at length. Professor

PORTRAIT OF HERZL AFTER J. KOPPAY, JERUSALEM, 1960. CAT. NO. 200

Herman Schapira, who unfortunately died soon after this Congress, submitted two proposals: one referring to the creation of a National Fund for the purchase of land in Palestine, the other dealing with the creation of a Jewish high school in Palestine.

The most important work accomplished by the First Congress was the establishment of a Jewish nation in Palestine, the main component of the Basel Program. Herzl later referred to this accomplishment in his diary: "In Basel I founded the Jewish State. If I were to say this today, I would be met by universal laughter. In five years, perhaps, and certainly in fifty, everyone will see it."

August 28, 1898–December 29, 1901
(Second–Fourth Congress)

Issues relating to the colonization of Palestine were first discussed in the Second Congress on August 28, 1898 in Basel. The most important question was whether the political Zionist organization should undertake colonization in Palestine before acquiring land through political concessions from the Turkish Government. A commission was appointed, and the following proposals were accepted by the Congress:

1. The first steps towards colonization should begin with the Jewish residents in the Turkish Empire. The political Zionist organization should obtain sanctions from the Turkish Government for such colonization.
2. A National Bank should be established to help aid the colonization process.
3. Herzl and a committee would survey the conditions in the existing colonies in Palestine.

Reporting on his political activities, Herzl told the Congress that he believed the negotiations with Constantinople looked positive and that he felt he would be able to obtain a meeting with the Kaiser during the latter's visit to the German colonies in Palestine in October.

On October 18, 1898, Herzl met informally with the German Emperor at Yildiz Kiosk, the residence of the Turkish Sultan. The Kaiser promised to exert influence on the Sultan to issue a charter for Zionist activities in Palestine.

Herzl's arrival in Palestine on October 26 was celebrated by the Jewish colonists. Ten days later, he had another informal meeting with the Kaiser at Mikveh Israel near Jaffa. Again, the Kaiser's tone appeared positive. Yet, when Herzl and the Kaiser met formally at German headquarters outside Jerusalem, the promise at Yildiz Kiosk was not publicly repeated.

When Herzl reported to the Third Congress in Basel, August 15–17 1899, he told of his encouraging meetings with the Kaiser. Hearing this promising news, delegates placed the responsibility for the diplomatic aspect of the Zionist movement on Herzl alone, and it remained that way until his death.

The Fourth Congress took place in London, August 13–16, 1900. Although the Jewish National Fund had been established in the First Congress, it did not take shape until 1901, immediately after the Fourth Congress. The collection of monies, to purchase and develop land in

Eretz Israel, soon began and the Fund grew rapidly.

Meanwhile, Herzl continued his diplomatic activities. On May 18, 1901, he was formally received by the Turkish Sultan, Abdul Hamid II, at Yildiz Kiosk, through the influential help of Armin Vabréy, a Jewish Professor of Oriental Languages at the University of Budapest, and language teacher to Princess Fatima, sister of the Sultan. Herzl was finally able to personally present his proposal to free Turkey of its debt in order to obtain friendly recognition of his cause from the Sultan, who assured Herzl that the Jews would continue to be in his favor under certain conditions. He promised that no harm would come to the Jews in the scattered settlements in Palestine as long as they would become Turkish citizens while immigrating. This automatically subjected the Jews to all Turkish laws, including military service. Although Herzl did not object immediately, he did not find the proposal acceptable, and planned to discuss it in the final negotiations. At the end of their meetings, the Sultan bestowed on Herzl the Grand Cordon of the Order of Medjidje, First Class.

December 29, 1901–July 3, 1904
(Fifth Congress until Herzl's Death)

The Fifth Congress in Basel, December 29–31, 1901, was marked by conflict. The Democratic Fraction criticized Herzl for his political views as well as for his lack of understanding of Jewish culture. Among this group were Ahad Ha-am, Martin Buber, and Chaim Weizmann. Furthermore, the religious contingents of the Zionist Organization—the Mizrachi—requested financial support as well as involvement in the Organization's activities. Herzl needed the backing of the large Mizrachi following, so he assured the subsidization of the Mizrachi in the Congress' budget. Another dispute involved Israel Zangwill's denouncement of the Jewish Colonization Association (I.C.A.) for its opposition to political Zionism.

In February 1902, the Sultan invited Herzl to participate in new negotiations with negative results. The Sultan offered colonization on land in Asia Minor and Iraq, but not in Palestine. He also demanded the creation of syndicates that would attend to all finances connected with immigration. Herzl refused, lacking the power to agree under such terms. Later he continued to negotiate with Constantinople, but the Turkish government eventually cut off talks for political reasons.

1902 was a politically active year for Herzl, but a sad one. As Jacob Herzl had provided a strong emotional and financial support to his son, his death in June was a harsh blow. But Herzl returned to his work in July, and he attended a conference in London with Lord Nathan Mayer Rothschild, who was very impressed with Herzl and attempted to arrange meetings with influential people such as Joseph Chamberlain, the colonial minister of the British government.

Herzl completed his last book, *Altneuland*, a Utopian vision of the future of the Jewish state. It is the story of a Jew who visits Palestine in 1898 and then returns 20 years later (1923). The barren land has disappeared and in its place are flourishing colonies; the country is now a cultural center where Jews and Arabs live peacefully together. In this book Herzl coined the famous,

"If you will it, it is no fairy tale." Unfortunately, *Altneuland* was not received positively, leading to even more trouble within the Zionist Organization. Many criticized the novel's lack of Jewish spirit and viewed it as a vain work of imagination.

After the long negotiations with the Turkish Sultan failed, a new plan arose to create a Jewish homeland in the province of El-Arish (located in the section of the Sinai desert bordering Palestine). The Sinai peninsula was politically controlled by the British and governed by Lord Cromer, the British consul-general in Egypt. With the help of Joseph Chamberlain, Lord Rothschild and an influential British Jew named Leopold Greenberg, El-Arish might have become a tangible refuge for Jewish immigrants from Eastern Europe.

In January 1903, with the approval of the Actions Committee, a delegation was sent to investigate the situation at El-Arish. Although some delegates were hesitant they approved the area. Herzl traveled to Cairo in March 1903 to discuss the project with Lord Cromer. Although he believed that he would only have to deal with the British, the Egyptians became very influential in the negotiations. On May 11, 1902, the Egyptian government gave their final refusal to the El-Arish plan.

The situation for Eastern European Jews was so rapidly deteriorating that Herzl desperately sought a refuge. He even took steps to approach the Portuguese government for a charter in Mozambique—the Belgian government for territory in the Congo, as well as the Italian government—for a section of Tripoli, but both of these countries eventually refused.

In August 1903, Herzl visited Russia, spurred by the tragedy of the Kishinev pogrom. Four months earlier, on April 3, 1903, groups of workers, peasants and city youths had attacked Jews in the Russian town of Kishinev. Forty-seven Jews were killed and 92 severely injured. The massacre shocked Jewish communities all over the world. Herzl hoped to visit Russian officials to discuss the pressing necessity for Jewish emigration. He wanted Russia's help in influencing Turkey to grant a charter for the start of a Jewish state. Herzl believed that his requests might be granted because of opportune timing; Russia was attempting to rebuild its international reputation after the Kishinev pogrom. Herzl easily arranged a meeting with the Adjutant General of the Tsar and two other powerful officials, Count Sergey Witte, Minister of Finance, and Wenzl von Plehve, Minister of the Interior (assassinated by revolutionaries in 1904).

Though Witte and Plehve were political opponents, they treated Herzl's views with fairness. Witte promised Herzl to end the prohibition on sales of shares for the National Jewish Bank, allowing Russian-Jews to contribute directly to the future Jewish State. Plehve appeared interested in Jewish emigration, though he refused to grant legal status to the Zionist organization in Russia. Plehve also delivered a communication in the name of the Tsar supporting plans to establish a Jewish commonwealth. Concerning Russia's help in influencing the Turks, Plehve gave an ambiguous answer. So Herzl left St. Petersburg without any tangible political promises, although Herzl had met with Jews to hear their suggestions, advice, and complaints.

When Herzl decided to visit the substantial Jewish community of Vilna, a tremendous reception there deeply moved him. Some people had walked great distances throughout the night simply to see him. The community house was packed with spectators and community leaders who praised him as "the greatest son of the Jewish people," and presented a symbol of their appreciation—a small Torah scroll. Herzl also visited the homes of poor Vilna Jews where the sight of their living conditions brought him to tears.

Deeply affected by the Jewish situation he had witnessed in Poland and Russia, Herzl opened the Sixth Zionist Congress on August 22. Aware that he could not find an immediate home for the Jews in Palestine, he sought temporary asylum in Uganda, under British protection, a plan previously developed by Joseph Chamberlain who had spoken with Herzl of the possibility of settling Jews in a part of a British possession in East Africa, in an area between Kenya and Uganda.

The Uganda plan divided the Sixth Zionist Congress. The Democratic Fraction and a large number of the Russian Jewish delegates flatly refuted the plan; they would not accept any land other than Palestine. Most of the Mizrachi supported Herzl because they understood the necessity of immediate Jewish immigration. When the issue was voted upon, 295 delegates were in favor, 178 were against, with 100 abstaining. The close vote sent the issues to the Greater Actions committee. Fearing an irreparable split in the Zionist organization, Herzl reassured the members that Palestine would not be forgotten. He ended the Sixth Congress with Psalm 137, v. 5 which he spoke in Hebrew, "If I forget thee, oh Jerusalem, may my right hand lose its cunning."

Herzl kept his word, never abandoning the hope of Palestine. In January of 1904, Herzl arrived in Italy; and he obtained an audience with King Victor Emmanuel III, who appeared sympathetic towards the Zionist cause. He told Herzl to wait to obtain Palestine once he had half a million Jews living there. Herzl pointed out that Jews were not even allowed in Palestine. Smiling, the king observed that anything can be done with *baksheesh* (bribery). (The seriousness of this statement is debatable.) Then, to decide the final amount of Italy's political support, the King directed Herzl to his Foreign Minister, Tuttoni, who proved to be of little help. Herzl also appeared before Pope Pius X who declared, "If you come to Palestine and settle your people there, we want to have churches and priests ready to baptize you."

A special meeting of the Greater Actions Committee was held on April 11 in Vienna. The potential Jewish homeland in East Africa was discussed again. Herzl sent an expedition to East Africa to explore the land. The delegation arrived at the end of June 1904 just when the rainstorms began. The heavy rains and the unfamiliar terrain proved so disconcerting that they returned to Europe immediately and the plan was dismissed.

After the rigorous debate on Uganda at the Congress, Herzl's health began to rapidly deteriorate. He had suffered from a heart condition all his adult life, but had paid little attention to it—his work was always of primary importance. In June 1904 he was admitted to the sanitarium at Edlach, near Vienna suffering from pneumonia. As his condition worsened, his family and close friends attended his bedside. On Sunday, July 3, 1904, he died. In his will he wished for a simple funeral, without speeches or flowers. However, the Jewish people could not contain their appreciation for Herzl's work. *Die Welt* estimated 6,000 mourners. Both Jewish and non-Jewish newspapers all over the US carried news of his death. In New York a memorial service was held on July

5, in the largest synagogue in the Lower East Side. Among the many who eulogized him was Dr. Joseph Bluestone. Memorial services were held throughout the country, including San Francisco, Boston, Denver and Washington, and American Jews mourned the passing of a great leader. In spite of the intense heat, the crowd moved from Herzl's home to the Deblinger cemetery. Everyone from the common people to prominent literary figures and politicians paid their respects to this great man. Herzl's death was mourned all over Eastern and Western Europe, where Jewish communities gathered to eulogize their beloved leader.

On August 18, 1949, one of the first acts of the new State of Israel was to bring Herzl's remains to Jerusalem for reburial on a hill later named Mount Herzl. This fulfilled one of Herzl's last requests—that he should be reinterred when the Jewish State became a reality.

Political Zionism in America During Herzl's Life

The Eastern European Jewish immigrants who arrived in the United States after the 1880-1881 Russian pogroms came from diverse social classes. Some brought their affiliation with the Hovevei Zion. Within this group were those who saw America as a temporary residence where they could learn a profession, such as agriculture and other technical trades, to later apply in Palestine. Small Zionist gatherings sprung up in large cities: New York, Chicago, Philadelphia, Baltimore, Milwaukee, Cincinnati, Boston and Cleveland.

Herzl's call for a Jewish State reached the American Zionists in 1896 with the publication of *The Jewish State*. Most of Hovevei Zion members looked favorably on Herzl's ideas, although a large group of American Jews opposed Herzl's views because of possible conflicts with their patriotism for the United States (a view shared similarly by some Western European Jews). In those years, American attitudes were not that crucial to Herzl's plan. His work was directed towards East Europeans whose social and economic situations were far worse than those of Jews in either Western Europe or America.

At the time of the First Congress in 1897, the Jewish population in America had reached one million. It is no wonder that the First Zionist Congress in Basel was attended by only four Americans, all affiliated with the American Zionist Organization. The general reaction to the Congress in the US can be gauged by the newspaper reports. *The New York Times* reported: "Dr. Herzl of Vienna has aroused in his country a deeper feeling than one of mere curiosity." A few days later the *Times* also reprinted an article from the *Chicagoer Israelit*:

> ...Don Quixote Herzl and Sancho Panza Nordau may be a queer sight but what are they to the mob which accepts them seriously—a mob composed of an element which now adds this folly to shame those upon whom they have been a burden. History has plenty of instances of ignorant Jews running after false Messiahs but there is no record of such stultification and wholesale revocation of all that had been previously sacred. The leaders and followers have equal reason for being proud of each other...

SHEET MUSIC, NEW YORK, EARLY 20TH CENTURY. CAT. NO. 15

A pro-Zionist report appeared in the *NY Sun* on August 31, 1897, and probably the warmest reception of the First Congress was offered by the *NY Tribune* on August 29, 1897:

> *The return of the Jews to Palestine is no longer to be regarded as an empty dream. Dream it was, through centuries of persecution...this month's convention at Basle, led by men such as Dr. Herzl and Max Nordau and participated in by representative Jews of all countries, must be regarded as something much more than a visionary.*

The Second Congress in Basel on August 28–30, 1898 was led by new, more distinguished American delegates: Prof. Richard Gottheil, the first Professor of Hebrew at Columbia University, and son of Reform Rabbi Gustav Gottheil of New York's Temple Emanuel, and young Reform Rabbi Stephen S. Wise of New York's Congregation B'nai Jeshurun.

At the First and Second Congress stimulated the interests of many American Jews. A number of Orthodox Jews, led by Rabbi Phillip Klein, supported Herzl's work on behalf of a Jewish commonwealth. American Jewish Zionists also demonstrated their support by purchasing many shares of the Jewish Colonial Bank and buying shekels. The Zionist movement also made an impact on individual Jewish families. All over the country, Jews from varying backgrounds held discussions and debates on the issues surrounding a Jewish homeland.

By the Third Congress in Basel in 1899, the number of American delegates had risen to 12, among them Prof. Gottheil and the well-known Sephardic Rabbi S. Solis-Cohen. By the Fourth Congress, 20 American delegates from the Zionist movement, plus a number of American spectators arrived in London. Five Americans were elected to the Greater Actions Committee, the leading body of the Zionist Organization. However, despite the optimistic appearance of American Jews in the Congress, Prof. Gottheil gave a disappointing account on the progress of Zionism in the United States. Out of one million American Jews, only 6,000 were registered members of the Zionist organization.

In the Fifth Congress Herzl made the following statement concerning American Jews:

> *"In the last few years a kind of so-called help, has indeed, been rendered, viz., the migration of the outcasts from Europe to the new world; in other words the discovery of America. Unhappily, this discovery came somewhat too late. America will have nothing more to do with these poor immigrants, just as little as England. Moreover, there is already too, in America, great Jewish suffering. And in America it has been emphatically recognized, that the solution we offer is the right one. As proof, see the growing number of Zionist associations which stretch in one long chain from the north of North America to the south of South America... ."*

In 1903, the Americans proposed a visit by Herzl to the United States where he could meet some of his American followers, but this never materialized. Herzl did correspond with a number of followers in the US among them the philanthropic millionaire Jacob Schiff, who could not visualize a Jewish state in Palestine, but felt that Palestine was needed as a refuge for immigrants and as a cultural and spiritual center. He admired Herzl's work and the two corresponded regularly. In fact, Herzl's last letter was written to Schiff.

To unite and educate the varying and diverse groups of the American Zionist Organization a national Zionist journal was needed. In October 1901, *The Maccabean*, a literary magazine in both Yiddish and English, was founded under editor Louis Lipsky. In 1902, Jacob de Haas, an emigre from London, and a close friend of Herzl, replaced Lipsky. In 1927, de Haas was to publish a two-volume biography on Herzl. *The Maccabean* remained the backbone of the American Zionist movement, until it ended publication in 1920.

During the Spring of 1903 a group of older, more religious Zionists broke away from the Federation of American Zionists to form the United Zionists, electing Rabbi Dr. Phillip Klein as their honorary president and Dr. I.J. Bluestone as permanent chairman. Their agenda:

1. Reaffirmation of the Basel Program
2. Support for Dr. Herzl
3. Endorsement of the Colonial Bank and the National Fund
4. Recruitment of American Jews for the Zionist cause

The trouble between the United Zionists and the FAZ continued into the Sixth Congress. When efforts by Herzl and Nordau to unite them failed, a conference of American Zionists was formed to work out an agreement.

The Sixth Congress was exceptionally controversial because of the Uganda issue. Herzl declared that his great effort to obtain Palestine through Turkey had broken down. The only other possibility was one offered by the English government—land in East Africa in Uganda. Herzl assured the Congress that Africa was far from his goal, but it was a temporary solution for immediate Jewish immigration until Palestine could be obtained. With the Congress in an uproar, the Russian delegates walked out, and the Americans debated furiously over the subject. In the end, the American vote was split. Richard Gottheil, Jacob de Haas, Cyrus Sulzberger, Leon Zolotkoff and Harry Friedenwald voted in favor of sending the Committee of Inquiry to Uganda. I.J. Bluestone and others of the United Zionists voted for the resolution.

Herzl's Family

Most of Herzl's private life was overshadowed by his public work. Although Herzl was devoted to his family, they were always second to his work. He married Julia Naschauer on July 25, 1889. She had been raised in a wealthy, social environment. In the beginning the Herzls enjoyed the life of a modern, prosperous couple. Julia was interested in society; Theodor was a promising writer. However, as Herzl became increasingly involved with the Jewish cause, he spent less and less time with his family. As most of his own wealth was spent on his diplomatic activities, his family was left with little means.

Herzl's family life dissolved tragically. Julia died a lonely woman in 1907 at age 39 convinced that the Zionist Movement had stolen her family. The deaths of the three Herzl children were even more sorrowful. Pauline, the eldest daughter, became drug-addicted and was treated at mental institutions for many years. In 1930, she died in Bordeaux from a heroin overdose. Hans, who was mentally unstable, converted to Christianity on the 20th anniversary of his father's death, and committed suicide a few days after Pauline's death. The youngest child, Trude, was unsuccessfully married to Richard Neumann. Their union produced a son, Stefan Theodor. Trude spent many years in the mental hospital of Steinhof near Vienna. When the Nazis occupied Austria, she was taken to the Theresienstadt concentration camp where she died in 1943. Herzl's line ended when Stefan Theodor killed himself in 1946.

Shlomo Eidelberg is Professor Emeritus of Jewish History, Stern College for Women, Yeshiva University.

SELECTED BIBLIOGRAPHY

1. Bein, A. *Theodor Herzl: A Biography*. Philadelphia, 1943.

2. de Haas, Jacob. *Theodor Herzl, A Bibographic Study*. 2 vols. Chicago, 1927.

3. Elon, A. *Herzl*. New York, 1975.

4. Feinstein, M. *American Zionism: 1884–1904*. New York, 1965.

5. Freidmann, A. *Das Leben Theodor Herzls* [German]. Berlin, 1919.

6. Friesel, A. *The Zionist Movement in the United States* [Hebrew]. Tel-Aviv, 1970.

7. Hertzberg, A. *The Zionist Idea*. New York, 1959.

8. Herzl, T. *Diaries*. New York, 1960.

9. Herzl, T. *The Jewish State*. New York, 1946.

10. Herzl, T. *Zionist Writings: Essays and Adresses (2 volumes)*. New York, 1973.

11. Nordau, Anna and Maxa. *Max Nordau: A Biography*. New York, 1943.

12. Patai, J. *Herzl*. [Hebrew]. Tel-Aviv, 1936.

13. Stewart, D. *Theodor Herzl*. New York, 1974.

14. Weisgal, M. *Theodor Herzl: A Memorial*. New York, 1929.

Dr. בנימין זאב הערצל על נהר רהיין.
נולד י"ד אייר שנת תר"כ — נפטר כ' תמוז תרס"ד.

Dr. Theodor Herzl an der Baseler Rheinbrücke.

Verlag „Zion", Wien, II/3.

Vienna

*Dec. 30
1904*

William H. Hechler

POSTCARD, VIENNA, 1904, AFTER 1901 PHOTOGRAPH BY E.M. LILIEN. CAT. NO. 174

Theodor Herzl: A Zionist Leader

Ruth A. Bevan

Viewed against his background, Theodor Herzl appears as an improbable Zionist leader. He did not carry his Jewish identity comfortably and wanted nothing more than to assimilate himself into genteel European society with its modern outlook. As the son of a successful banker, he enjoyed the privileges of a comfortable bourgeois life, being something of a "dandy" and a "snob." He disdained and disassociated himself from Jews who, in his estimation, were not "modern." Yet, this complex man revolutionized world Jewry and its destiny. In creating the world Zionist movement in 1895, Theodor Herzl gave reality to the centuries-old dream of Jews to return to their homeland. Zion, the land of Israel, from which the Jews had been exiled by the ancient Romans in the year 70, is that homeland which they continued to remember in their daily prayers.

Theodor Herzl was born on May 2, 1860 in the Danubian town of Pest, Hungary. Thirteen years later, Pest united with Buda and Obuda to form the vibrant city of Budapest, the second major metropolis after Vienna in the Austro-Hungarian empire. Theodor's maternal grandparents had migrated to Pest from the Austrian province of Moravia, and his mother cultivated in him a love of German culture. This lifelong Germanophilism induced in Herzl an early sympathy for German nationalism. He admired Bismarck and, as a university student in Vienna, joined the German nationalist Fraternity (*Burschenschaft*) "Albia." Even dueling was attractive to him as a means to defend one's honor.

In 1868, after the death of his sister, Herzl's family moved to Vienna. The move may have been in response to the Magyar nationalism reverberating throughout Pest since the Protestant Lajos Kossuth ignited the 1848 revolution there against Habsburg control. By contrast, the German-speaking Catholic inhabitants of Buda were Habsburg loyalists. Herzl's parents clearly felt themselves more at home in Vienna and, perhaps, more secure as well.

Herzl's drive to assimilate reflected the spirit of Jewish emancipation in his time. In spreading French revolutionary values across Europe, Napoleon held out to Jews the amazing prospect of equal citizenship rights. The old ghetto walls began to crumble. Herzl grew up in the feverish excitement of this emancipation. He was seven years old when Jews acquired civic rights in his native Hungary. Influenced by the *Haskalah* (Enlightenment), his parents firmly believed that Jews should "modernize" themselves in order to become "worthy citizens." They sent Herzl to schools, including a Jewish primary school, with a modern curriculum. His boyhood "hero" was the modern figure, Ferdinand de Lesseps, who built the Suez Canal. In his youth he dreamed of becoming a writer, not a Zionist leader, and living a free life in his beloved Vienna. Assimilation, he believed, was "progressive," and would, as he implicitly assumed, end anti-semitism.

Herzl's biographer, Steven Beller, points out the paradox in this acculturation process of newly emancipated Jews. As they assimilated via similar social and professional routes, they remained identifiable as Jews. Journalism, Herzl's career choice attracted many Jews. Herzl thus became a "typically" assimilated Viennese bourgeois Jew. Ironically, assimilation failed to melt down the barriers between Jews and non-Jews. Consequently, it, failed to extinguish anti-semitism.

The persistence of anti-semitism, despite Jewish emancipation, shocked Herzl to the core. He suffered his own painful experiences with this "disease." One experience, in particular, profoundly affected him. When a total stranger hurled an anti-semitic slur at him in the street, Herzl was deeply troubled and came to a startling realization: Jews are discernible as a physical "type." Despite his cultural assimilation, his physical appearance, notably his darker complexion, betrayed his "difference." Rather than solving the "Jewish question," emancipation had actually produced a new form of anti-semitism. Those now opposed to the emerging industrial order targeted Jews as the driving force behind a variety of ideological "isms" operating within this order—liberalism, capitalism (urban industrialism), socialism and communism. Such an identification later constituted the core of Nazi anti-semitism.

A Lesson in Assimilation

Herzl witnessed the explosion of this modern anti-semitism in the Dreyfus Affair in France. Accused of betraying French military secrets to Germany, Captain Alfred Dreyfus, an Alsatian French Jew, went on trial in December 1894. Herzl reported on the trial for the Viennese *Neue Freie Presse*, for which he was the Paris correspondent, 1891–1895. The court found Dreyfus guilty and exiled him to Devil's Island. Herzl was present at the degradation of Captain Dreyfus on January 5, 1895. Later, Emile Zola, the renowned writer, accused the French army of a cover-up to protect the real culprit, Major Esterhazy, who, in 1897 had been tried on the same charges as Dreyfus but then acquitted. Popular demand led to a reopening of the case. In 1899 Dreyfus was retried and pardoned. Anti-Dreyfusards had used anti-semitism for their own political purposes; they hoped to discredit liberal republicanism, arguing that civic equality permits Jews like Dreyfus to break into professions, such as the army's officer corps, once reserved for the aristocracy.

In Paris, Herzl realized the futility of his own assimilation efforts. While he blended more easily into the Parisian crowds, where his Mediterranean complexion was not that unusual, he, nevertheless, had his own unpleasant brushes with anti-semitism. He now understood that Vienna had no monopoly on anti-semitism. The Dreyfus Affair aptly demonstrated that liberal Paris mirrored imperial Vienna in its prejudice against Jews. In his play, *The New Ghetto*, written three months before the Dreyfus trial, Herzl depicts emancipated Jews as living in a new ghetto of "invisible walls."

Ironically, Herzl's very attempts to assimilate made him more conscious of the intractability of anti-semitism. Had he been a less assimilated Jew, he would, no doubt, have taken anti-semitism more for granted, assuming it to be a possible consequence of his Jewish "difference." Herzl, however, tried to eliminate such a difference in himself so he would be "like others." Unable to achieve this "likeness," he flung himself in the opposite direction. Now he resolved to emphasize his "difference" through separation. Assimilation, like an unrequited love, was no longer worth the effort.

In April 1895 Herzl discussed with a Parisian friend his desire to write a book "about the Jews." Following the friend's suggestion to cast his ideas as a novel, Herzl proceeded to redraft an old manuscript of his, a novel, entitled, Samuel Kohn. He added a new ending in which the hero's friend finds the Promised Land. Intrigued by the implications of his own fantasy, Herzl abandoned the novel and set about writing a practical plan for Jews to secure their own homeland and, excited by the results, impetuously sent a copy of his plan to Baron de Hirsch, a prominent Jewish banker and philanthropist. That inspired letter won Herzl an interview with the baron on June 2. This meeting marks the "start of Herzl's Zionism," for revisions of the original plan presented to the baron quickly resulted in the finished manuscript of Herzl's tide-tuning Zionist tract, *Der Judenstaat.*[1]

In Paris, Herzl's long, inner struggle with his own identity resolved itself. Returning to Vienna in April 1895 to assume the post of *feuilleton* editor of the *Neue Freie Presse*, Herzl left Paris as a Zionist. Having had his "moment of truth" he now presented Julia, the woman he had married six years earlier, and his three children with a radically new direction in life.

Years later, in recalling his Paris interlude to the young writer Stefan Zweig, whom Herzl met in Vienna, he exclaimed: "Everything I know, I learnt abroad. Only there does one get used to thinking in distances. I am convinced that here I would never have had the courage to formulate that first conception. Somebody would have nipped it in the bud before it had a chance to grow. But thank G-d, when I brought it here, it was already complete, and they could do nothing but cock a leg."[2]

Der Judenstaat ("The Jews' State") was published on February 14, 1896. Herzl subtitled it, "An Attempt at a Modern Solution to the Jewish Problem." Within the 80 page pamphlet, he developed three main ideas: the need for united leadership among Jews, the need to improve the "national character" of Jews and the need to form a "movement" to create a state where Jews can govern themselves. Herzl entertained no illusions about the amount of preparation that would be required for this exodus from "Egypt," which he anticipated would take place within 40 years. As he envisioned it, a congress of notables, composed of representatives from Jewish communities, would plan the exodus.

True to his values, Herzl conceived the Jews' state as a secular "aristocratic republic." Of necessity, in view of the Jews' world-wide dispersion, this republic would be multicultural as well as multilingual, Hebrew not being the official language. Importantly, the state would be ultramodern, improving upon European technology as well as advancing its scope of social legislation (e.g., through measures like the seven hour work day), of paramount concern to Herzl who, interestingly, inclined toward socialism. In building a "new world," Jews would be morally rejuvenated and become a "light unto the nations." With Hegelian-style reasoning, Herzl projected the Jews' state as a preeminent world actor, its special mission being to demonstrate to the world the meaning of tolerance. In an August 1899 diary entry, Herzl notated his testament to the Jews: "Make your state so that the stranger feels at ease among you."[3]

The basic premise of Herzl's Zionism is that Jews are a *nation*. Anti-semitism, in Herzl's mind, confirmed the separate nationality of the Jews. If Jews are a nation, then why shouldn't they have their own state? This question caught the spirit of the age, for national struggles were dramatically impacting upon the international state system. The Magyar revolt of 1848 brought Hungary substantial home rule and a leadership role next to Austria in the empire. Bismarck unified Germany. In the New World, South American colonies had already achieved statehood by 1822. And, of course, there were the "revolutionary patriarchs," France and the United States, the latter of special interest to Herzl.

At a time when emancipated Jews sought to integrate themselves into the national cultures of their various "host" countries, Herzl's concept of a "Jewish nation" engendered resistance. Would these "hosts" now look upon the Jews as "a nation within a nation?" Would Jews, thereby, be suspected of divided loyalties? Would integration into their respective "host nations," consequently, be jeopardized? Moreover, not all Jews accepted Herzl's pessimistic assessment of anti-semitism, which many felt had "died down" after the Dreyfus Affair.

Isaiah Berlin, the renowned contemporary British intellectual historian, faults Herzl for being too categorical in his assessment of anti-semitism, arguing that Herzl underestimated the potential of liberal democracy to raise its tolerance level.[4] While this criticism has merit, Herzl did not witness the maturity of the liberal democratic principle in his lifetime—despite Benjamin Disraeli's success in opening up English parliamentary membership to Jews and the decline of anit-semitism in France after the Dreyfus Affair. Had Herzl, however, not been categorical, he never would have been moved to build the Zionist movement. His "error" forever changed Jewish and world history. His "error" also proved fortuitous in view of the cataclysmic events in Russia (1917) and Germany (1933) which added cultural and physical genocide to the meaning of the "Jewish problem."

The Idea of Zionism

Self-absorbed, Herzl remained remarkably ignorant of other Zionists of his time, like Moses Hess, Leo Pinsker, and Nachman Syrkin, who had, after all, achieved intellectual prominence. Although a novelist, he never even read, according to Beller, George Eliot's acclaimed Zionist novel *Daniel Deronda*. Herzl thought he had invented Zionism and was shocked to learn otherwise. Of course, no nineteenth century Zionist could aggregate such credit unto himself, for the Zionist legacy stretched back centuries. (Jewish emancipation, however, had prompted a Zionist resurgence.) Upon finally reading Pinsker's influential work, *Autoemancipation*, which called for the immediate exodus of Jews from Europe, Herzl, dumbfounded, remarked that, had he read Pinsker's book, he might not have written *Der Judenstaat*. His unfamiliarity with other Zionist thinkers imbued Herzl, however, with a sense of his own prophetic genius and "mission."

Herzl believed in the power of ideas. More particularly, he understood, like Nietzsche, the driving power of will. In the epilogue of his *Altneuland* (1902), a fantasy novel about the "new Zion," he penned: "If you will it, it is no fable." His imposing good looks, princely bearing and eloquence prevented his autocratic will from deterring others; instead it inspired. No other Zionist commanded such support. For Europe's demoralized Jews, this assimilationist turned iconoclast pulsated as the "New Jew" of a shining tomorrow. Herzl's ability to forge a united Zionist movement out of disparate groups might well be likened, despite obvious ideological and stylistic differences, to Karl Marx's. Herzl's *Der Judenstaat* transformed the Zionist cause as Marx's *Communist Manifesto* of 1848 transformed the socialist cause.

Herzl was not, however, a rough, anti-establishment revolutionary like Marx, for he needed to contract territory for the Jews' state from major power holders of the world. Trained as a lawyer (a profession he abandoned for journalism), Herzl insisted that land be procured through just deeds and recompense. If Palestine were to be the Jewish homeland, then the Ottomans were to be involved. To persuade the Ottomans, Herzl would need international support. Herzl entered the world of international diplomacy, taking Zionism into the royal courts of Europe from 1896 until 1902. He gained initial entry through an Anglican clergyman, William Hechler, who introduced him to Friedrich, Grand Duke of Baden. The Polish nobleman, Philip de Nevlinski, paved the way to the Ottoman court in Constantinople. Herzl met twice with Kaiser Wilhelm II in Constantinople and again at a Rothschild colony in Palestine. The Kaiser seemed willing to make the Jewish homeland a German protectorate. Complications arose, and the scheme fell apart. Nevertheless, Herzl persevered, making "Zionism, almost single-handedly, a player in international diplomacy." [5]

Herzl also understood the power of mass politics in the democratic age. He had learned this lesson in Paris where his reporting assignments forced him to come to grips with democratic organizational politics, He did not like politics, but the political skills he mastered in those Paris years proved indispensable to his Zionist work. His elitist inclinations notwithstanding, Herzl proceeded to mobilize the Jewish masses behind his Zionist ideas. Zionism had to become a "movement" (perhaps he took his cue from the German Jewish Social Democratic leader, Ferdinand Lassalle, whom he admired).

Faced with a Zionistically enthusiastic "mass," the Jewish establishment would be forced to listen. He began a mass campaign to raise money and founded a Zionist weekly, *Die Welt* (1897). His insistence on having a Zionist flag around which individuals could rally and for which they would die, if need be, showed his acute understanding of mass psychology, as did his fantasy novel, *Altneuland* (1902), which fired aspirations for the "new Zion."

The Congress Realized

His will, charisma, and vision created the magic that made possible the groundbreaking First Zionist Congress, held in the Swiss city of Basel at the elegant Stadt Casino from August 29–31, 1897. It was the congress envisioned in *Der Judenstaat*. Assembled were 204 delegates from 15 countries, including the United States. To create a "civilized" atmosphere at the Congress, Herzl stipulated that all delegates should come in white tie attire. Feeling "stiff" in their formal clothing, the delegates, Herzl reasoned, would sense that Zionism was not leading them into a desert, but into a higher civilization, and would conduct themselves with civilized forbearance.

With his opening speech, Herzl electrified the delegates. "We want to lay the cornerstone," he said, "of the edifice which is one day to house the Jewish nation." Afterwards, Max Nordau, a well known physician and author, who was now Herzl's second-in-command, delivered a fiery speech about the "moral misery" of emancipated Jewry. Nordau (who had connected Herzl with important English Jews like Sir Moses Montefiore) skillfully engineered the delegates' unanimous acceptance of the Basel Program, a statement of political Zionist objectives. "Zionism," it asserted, "seeks to secure for the Jewish people a publicly recognized, legally secured homeland in Palestine." Toward the end of the Congress, the World Zionist Organization was established as the political instrument of world Jewry "on the way to independence." [6] At the end of the Congress, "thunderous applause greeted Herzl...." [7]

His heart weakened seriously after the First Congress, Herzl was advised by doctors to rest. Nevertheless, he continued to work. With his establishment of the Jewish National Fund, set up to purchase land in Palestine, at the Fifth Congress in 1901, all the major organizational machinery of the Zionist movement was in place. In 1904, the year of his death, he met with Italy's King Victor Emmanuel III. His heart condition steadily deteriorating, Theodor Herzl succumbed on July 3, 1904 at the untimely age of 44. Crowds gathered to commemorate the Zionist leader who had revolutionized Jewish history. Three years later, his wife died at the age of 39. His three children met tragic, premature deaths. The youngest, Trude, met her fate in Theresienstadt in 1943.

Herzl was the last of an era. When he died, the liberal age was closing. Mazzini, another liberal national leader, had died, as an exile in England in 1872, profoundly disappointed that the unified republican Italy for which he had fought had, instead, become a unified kingdom. Already in Herzl's lifetime, central European ethno-nationalism was taking a turn toward "ethnic purity" after the failed "springtime of nations" revolutions in 1848. Herzl's letters indicate that he had premonitions about the future consequences of this turn. Ultimately, the Nazis transformed the meaning of nationalism into racism.

Other New Worlds

The New World offered Herzl more inspiration than the Old. Believing that Zionists would build a "new world," he found an example in the social experimentation of the United States. South America, liberated by Simon Bolivar and Jose San Martin, presented a similar potential for innovation. At an early stage, Herzl had seriously considered Argentina as a possible Jewish colonization site After Herzl's death, American Jews immeasurably fortified the Zionist movement. South American Jews became the movement's largest per-capita donors.

In comparing Herzl with New World liberal nationalist leaders, noticeable differences emerge. Unlike George Washington or Simon Bolivar (the "George Washington of Latin America"), Herzl was no military figure. He fought no war of independence. His concern was not to oust a colonial power but to contract land. He also never became a power holder in his new land, not even living to see it established.

The New World leader who provides an interesting resemblance to Herzl is Juan Pablo Duarte y Diez, father of the Dominican Republic. Duarte was born on January 26, 1813, in Santo Domingo. His father was a successful Spanish businessman, who had also been prominent in public affairs. His mother was Dominican. As a young man, he lived for some time in Barcelona, Spain, where he absorbed European manners and the new liberalism. These Barcelona years were as pivotal for Duarte as the Paris years were for Herzl. Duarte returned to Santo Domingo bent upon freeing his homeland from French Haitian control, in effect since 1822, and also insisted upon separation from Spain, a novel policy at the time. His intent was to build a Dominican Republic (he gave the name to the new state) which would be "a genuine expression of the unity of all Dominican social groups, regardless of political belief or skin color." [8] The flag he chose, whose blue and red quadrants were defined by the arms of a white cross, symbolized the "union of all the races for the furtherance of civilization of Christianity." [9]

Thanks to Duarte's "la Trinitaria," a secret society devoted to Dominican independence, Haitain occupation ended in 1844. His life in jeopardy, Duarte was out of the country at the time, returning two weeks after the Haitians left, and was "received upon his arrival as the nation's idol." [10] Spontaneously and popularly proclaimed president, he insisted upon an election. Duarte, however, never became president. A *junta* usurped power and immediately exiled him.

Prior to his departure, Duarte comforted and counseled some supporters: "Be happy, citizens of Puerta Plata, and my heart will be fully satisfied even without the office which you desire I may obtain, but first of all, be just, if you desire to be happy, for that is man's first duty; be united...so shall I obtain my greatest recompense, the only one to which I aspire: that of seeing you peaceful, happy, independent and free." [11] In his classic history of the Dominican Republic, Sumner Welles concluded that "in the long line of patriots of the Americas who lived and, often, died that the creed of liberty might not perish from the New World, Duarte will ever hold an eminent place." [12]

Evolution of a Nation

After the first Basel Congress, Herzl wrote in his diary: "I would say, in Basle I created the Jewish state. Were I to say this aloud I would be greeted by universal laughter. But perhaps five years hence, in any case, certainly 50 years hence, everyone will perceive it." [13] On September 1, 1947, just 50 years after that diary entry, the United Nations Special Commission on Palestine recommended Jewish sovereignty in partitioned Palestine. In keeping with his wishes, Theodor Herzl's remains were removed from their Vienna resting place and flown to Israel where, on August 18, 1949, he was buried on Mount Herzl.

What distinguished Herzl's political Zionism was its liberal inclusiveness. Ideologically, it was not directed at any particular Jewish group or class but pertained to all Jews—believers and skeptics, capitalists and workers. It was truly a *national* concept, and this was the source of its strength and success. Few of the organizational particulars Herzl detailed in *Der Judenstaat* came to fruition; they weren't the issue. Even the idea of Jews returning to their homeland found precedence. The crucial difference in Herzl's Zionism was the revolutionary idea that Jews had the implicit right *as a nation* to their own state, that the implementation of this right demanded international negotiations for the legal procurement of territory, and that a massive Jewish exodus could, in fact, be organized.

Herzl did encounter serious dissension in his movement. The Russian contingent wanted a more substantial Jewish orientation. Ahad Ha-Am (Arthur Ginsberg, who was associated with Pinsker) spoke for these so-called "culturalists" (with whom Martin Buber and Chaim Weizmann were affiliated) who wanted more emphasis put on developing the Hebrew language. The disagreement between Herzl and the culturalists raised the essential question of Zionism still relevant today. Is Zionism the attempt to give Jews a safe haven where they can be like other nations? Or, is Zionism the attempt to promote a Jewish cultural-religious renaissance?

The answer appears to be, "both." As evidenced by "Operation Magic Carpet" in 1949–1950 which brought Yemenite Jews to Israel as well as the ingathering of Ethiopian and Russian Jews in the 1980s, Israel today remains a haven for persecuted Jews. Israel's present day reality corresponds to Herzl's hopes—a multicultural, multilingual modern society (with Hebrew, however, as the official language) in which a distinct Israeli national personality has developed. Furthermore, Israel is an international actor like other states.

Yet, the Zionist dynamic has been shifting with the increasing numbers of religious Jews in Israel. Political Zionism appears on the wane, perhaps because its objective of securing the state has been fulfilled. Menachem Begin, the Israeli prime minister who shared a Nobel Peace prize with Anwar Sadat for the Israeli-Egyptian peace agreement, combined religious with political Zionism. An orthodox Jew, he was also a disciple of Ze'ev Jabotinsky (born in Odessa in 1880), leader of the so-called Revisionists who considered themselves the heirs of Herzl. After the Balfour Declaration of 1917, the Revisionists pushed for massive immigration to Palestine so that Jews would come to constitute a majority in their "homeland" and thereby assume sovereign control. They also urged the cultivation of diplomatic grand alliances to facilitate independence. After being elected prime minister in 1977, Begin hung Jabotinsky's picture next to Herzl's in his office.

The "culturalists," insisting upon Palestine as the land of settlement, scored a decisive victory over Herzl. While Herzl had himself favored Palestine from early on in his Zionist career, he entertained other possible sites as stop-gap measures. In 1903, Chamberlain of England offered Uganda to Herzl as territory for Jewish settlement. Having turned down a similar offer in 1902, Herzl now decided to negotiate. Pogroms in Russian (e.g., Kishinev in April 1903) made the "Jewish quotation" urgent. Political calculations figured in. In negotiating, Herzl allegedly hoped to curry favor with England, a major force in the Middle East, and to win a bargaining token with the Turks. His risky decision to negotiate rebounded. While the majority of delegates at the Sixth Congress of 1903 supported Herzl (295–177), the entire opposition, including most of the Russians, walked out after the vote. If he were to save the movement, Herzl had to capitulate. In a dramatic act of reconciliation, Herzl, before the entire Congress, raised his right hand and proclaimed, "If I forget you, O Jerusalem, let my right hand wither." (Psalm 137.5)

Herzl knew, and expressed in writing, his own historical significance. This "tall individual with a princely Assyrian beard" was already a legend in his own time.[14] Whatever his human frailties, Herzl conducted himself as *the* Zionist leader with utmost integrity. He was committed to the cause, not to power. Emphasizing that the means used to achieve a Jewish homeland must be legal and responsible, he earned the international respectability and admiration for Zionism that facilitated its success. His obvious historical significance lies in this accomplishment. It is, however, not his only legacy. The *quality* of his leadership, his own character, further ennobled his cause.

Theodor Herzl was not a narrowly partisan national leader. In speaking for Jews, he never forgot the rights and needs of others. In uplifting Jews, he dreamed about a better world for all humanity. In the end, Theodor Herzl will be remembered for his faith in the ability of the human spirit to create the seemingly impossible—if we *will* it.

Ruth A. Bevan is the occupant, David W. Petegorsky Chair in Political Science, Yeshiva University.

FOOTNOTES

1. Steven Beller. *Herzl*. London. Weidenfeld & Nicolson. 1991, p, 33.

2. Stefan Zweig. *Die Welt von Gestern*. Frankfurt/Main. Fischer. 1970. pp. 131–2. Quoted in Steven Beller. *Herzl*. London. Weidenfeld & Nicolson. 199 1. p. II.

3. Herzl. *Briefe und Tagebuecher*. Vol. 2. p. 43. Quoted in Beller. *ibid.* p. 83.

4. In another vein, the Russian *Bund* of the 1880s argued that a socialist Europe, promoting egalitarianism, would solve the "Jewish problem," obviating the need for a Jewish state.

5. Beller. op. *cit.* p.65.

6. Monty Noam Penkower. *The Emergence of Zionist Thought*. Millwood, N.Y. Associated Faculty Press, Inc. 1986. p. 47.

7. *ibid.* p. 48.

8. Juan D. Balcacer y Manuel A. Garcia. *La Independencia Dominicana*. Editoreal MAPFRE. 1982. p. 76.

9. *ibid.* p. 77.

10. Sumner Welles. *Naboth's Vineyard: The Dominican Republic, 1844–1924*. Mamaroneck, N.Y. Paul P. Appel. 1966. vol. 1. p. 63.

11. *ibid.*, p. 75.

12. *ibid.*, p. 72.

13. Penkower. *op. cit*, p. 52.

14. *ibid.*, p. 48.

POSTCARD, VIENNA, BEFORE 1949. ARTIST: S. KRETSCHMER. CAT. NO. 23

Theodor Herzl: Zionist Symbol

Bonni-Dara Michaels

This exhibition consists of a selection from the more than one thousand pieces of Herzl memorabilia from the collection of Manfred Anson. They provide a window through which we can visualize the immense popularity of Theodor Herzl during and after his lifetime, at the same time that we retrace his single minded quest to create a national Jewish homeland.

The nature of the Anson collection of necessity shaped Yeshiva University Museum's exhibition. Mr. Anson's perspective on Herzl is that of a continuing historical narrative of people and events. He will keep an audience spellbound as he recounts the story of Herzl's life, the Congresses, Herzl's early death from illness and overwork, and the work of the Zionist movement, reaching a climax with the creation of the State of Israel. He perceives the Zionist movement as commencing with Theodor Herzl, continuing through the Congresses, the Jewish National Fund, early Israeli banks, and other organizations which financed and kept the movement alive, and those which promoted and supported pioneer life in Eretz Israel. Historical landmarks along the route to the creation of the State of Israel also find a place in this collection, including material commemorating the Balfour Declaration and the declaration of the State of Israel. For Manfred Anson, each item in his collection represents a tangible link with history.

His collection is ecclectic, including items of disparate sizes and media, and including much that is commonly known as ephemera and decorative arts. Manfred avidly collects any artifact decorated with Herzl's image, or bearing the quotation, "If you will it, it is not a dream." He also collects pieces which depict famous individuals who helped Herzl achieve his dream, such as David Wolffsohn and Max Nordau. Items depicting individuals who Herzl hoped would aid his cause, such as Kaiser Wilhelm, are also represented in this collection. Political and military leaders in Eretz Israel after Herzl's death, such as Chaim Weizmann and Joseph Trumpeldor, find a place in the Anson collection in the form of medals, plaques and postcards. Biographies of Herzl, plays, essays and books written by Herzl, and books on Zionism and famous Zionists are also represented in this collection.

These artifacts exhibit diverse uses of Herzl's image, the manner in which this image changed over time while retaining its significance as the expression of an ideological viewpoint, and the continuing vitality of this image into our time. Visiting a highly personal collection like this one also enables visitors to perceive the excitement of the collector's own hunt for artifacts, and to marvel at the diligence and passion with which he pursued his search.

Several factors shaped the nature of the exhibited artifacts. Technological innovations in photography during the nineteenth century made possible the documentation of Herzl's social and political life and his work for the Zionist cause. Portraits of Herzl, his activities and family were easily and inexpensively reproduced in postcards and books, and copied in other media. In the same era, journalism became increasingly important as a tool for informing and manipulating public opinion. This trends helped spread information about contemporary national and political movements, including Zionism.

Herzl himself began a journalistic career in Vienna, serving on the staff of the liberal *Neue Freie Presse*, reporting mainly his impressions and observations on various European cities. As a correspondent for the *Neue Freie Presse*, he was present at the Dreyfus trial in Paris which made a strong and lasting impression on this sophisticated, assimilated Jew.

During the Victorian era, the home was the place for inculcating proper attitudes and behavior in family members. Through home decoration, a family displayed their commitment to aesthetics, as well as to political and social trends. Previously, some Jewish families hung images of revered religious personalities in their homes. Now, as the century drew to a close, portraits of popular Zionist leaders who promised another sort of redemption joined this august company. A plethora of objects in textiles, metal, wood and ceramic decorated with Herzl's image was one manifestation of the fashionable Victorian-era vogue for collecting and displaying various types of decorative and often non-functional objects.

The popularity of the nascent Zionist movement is demonstrated by the variety of commercial objects it engendered—particularly during the first half of the 20th century—in the form of souvenirs and postcards, which offered distributors the chance to profit while spreading group propaganda. The image of Herzl became the quintessential Zionist icon, symbolizing the ideology and aims of political Zionism.

A handsome, statuesque gentleman, Herzl dressed as befitted a member of the European bourgeoisie; his vigorous physique provided a strong contrast to the prevailing stereotype of the *shtetl* Jew. Until the establishment of the State of Israel, Herzl's image was the preeminent symbol of the aspiration for Jewish statehood, accorded a place of honor in Jewish homes, particularly in Russia and Poland. In 1948 when David Ben Gurion proclaimed the State of Israel, he stood under a portrait of Herzl. Thereafter, Herzl's image suffered a decline in popularity, superseded by images of heroes and heroines of the new nation including Golda Meir and Moshe Dayan. However, the pattern had been set; Herzl was viewed as the father of Israel. To this day, when multiple portraits are chosen to portray the panoply of Jewish leaders and heroes throughout time, Herzl is among them, often positioned in relation to other figures in a manner expressive of his preeminence.

In 1901, Martin Buber addressed the Third Zionist Congress, promoting the use of art as a vehicle for Zionist education and propaganda. He believed that art could provide expression for Jewish nationalism. The traditional media of that time—painting, graphics and sculpture—were joined by the increasingly common use of photography. All four were employed to spread the doctrine of Zionism clearly and simply. To this day, the image of Herzl retains its power to stir those familiar with the history of Israel, an evocative icon which continually reminds us of the creation of the Jewish State.[1]

The Anson collection affords an opportunity to explore the Zionist iconography—the traditional symbols and images of the Zionist movement. By interpreting Zionism through the Anson collection, we discover how certain common objects located in the home create the context for understanding the development and maintenance of a new cultural identity during the hundred years of the Zionist movement from the time of the First Zionist Congress. While these items do not map a chronological story of Herzl and Zionism, they bring the visitor closer to Herzl and the Zionist movement as experienced by the majority of its adherents since its inception. Perhaps the most common form of this experience was the purchase, exchange and display of items with Zionist images. These items demonstrate the extent to which Herzl was (and still is) central to the self-definition of Zionist organizations, and to that of the State of Israel itself.

Beginning with the First Congress, Herzl employed popular art (primarily in the form of postcards and delegate badges) to present arguments about Zionism in a manner that was simple and easy to grasp. He used a ritualized ceremony (the Congresses themselves) to both disseminate and advance the Zionist cause, demonstrating his grasp of political theater.

The early Zionist imagery presents Eretz Israel as both old and new homeland, refuge for all its people who required sanctuary, and de-emphasizes the conflict between traditional religious Jews and secular Jewish nationalism. Images of Herzl himself were used like an icon by Zionist organizations and eventually by the State of Israel to symbolize Zionist claims and authority. Such images provided Jews throughout the world with a locus of access to Zionism in the same manner that religious icons traditionally provide a locus of access to the divine. Herzl's image was also adopted for commercial purposes by individuals and firms wishing to profit from the associations evoked by his image, and much of the unattributed body of material probably belongs to this category. Like relics, Herzl's body and personal possessions were enshrined, exploited first by the Zionist organizations, especially the Jewish National Fund (JNF), and then by the State of Israel, to provide a direct link to their origins at the time and under the auspices of Herzl.

The nineteenth century was a period of emerging nationalism, during which groups recognized their own collective value and distinct cultural history. This fostered a strong desire for independence among various groups, resulting in the fragmentation of the map of Europe into nation states, each with its own language, culture and proud history. Initially, many Jews viewed nationalism as a first step towards emancipation in those areas in which they had not yet received full rights as citizens. It was believed that all people would soon be equal in the rising community. But the rising tide of anti-semitism in France, Austria, Germany, Russia (Poland) and Romania, dispelled this illusion. Jews of Western Europe were able to enjoy comfortable lives despite outbreaks of anti-semitism, but pogroms in Russia-Poland made life intolerable for Jews in Eastern Europe. It was obvious that a solution had to be found. Theodor Herzl established a blueprint for Zionist leadership and activism which would culminate in the establishment of the State of Israel.

Ever since the destruction of the Temple, first in 586 B.C.E. and then in 70 C.E., the Jewish people prayed for a return to Zion (Eretz Israel) and the restoration of their homeland. Herzl became a hero for fashioning the political Zionist movement, restoring the Jews' self image as a great and powerful nation, its members working together to realize the dream of a Jewish homeland where Jews no longer needed to suffer anti-semitism. Herzl gave Jews a sense of themselves as a nation, regardless of where individuals resided or the individual's level of religious observance. A charismatic leader and a good organizer, he possessed a strong sense of drama that was appreciated by his contemporaries. He won a place in the hearts of the Jewish people as an admired leader, redeemer, and guardian of his people: the hero who laid down his life for their sake.

Two aspects of the existence of Theodor Herzl can be examined through artifacts and especially through Zionist imagery: one historical, the other more cultic and mythical. Items in the Anson collection reveal aspects of both.

In 1896, Herzl published *Der Judenstaat* (The Jewish State) in which he set forth his ideas for the creation of a Jewish homeland, and the economic labor and technological skills necessary to maintain it. Such a homeland, he reasoned, would permit Jews to escape anti-Semitism without assimilation or conversion from Judaism. So popular was this work that it was translated into five languages (including Russian, English and French) during the next year.

Herzl's life as author and playwright is well-represented in this collection. An autographed first edition of *Der Judenstaat* [cat. no. 2], published in 1896, sets forth Herzl's ideas for the creation of a Jewish homeland, and the types of work and technological knowledge necessary to maintain it.

Herzl orchestrated and chaired the First Zionist Congress, held in Basel in 1897. This brought together Jewish representatives from around the world. Herzl took advantage of the nascent explosion of visual material. Postcards were made to convey central concepts of his Zionist agenda. There were several basic images expressing Zionist ideology and aspirations, and the nationalist spirit. One of the basic themes of Zionist iconography was an idealistic expression of life in Eretz Israel, the national homeland. A souvenir postcard from the Second Zionist Congress juxtaposes figures praying at the Western Wall with a pioneer working in the fields against a rising sun [cat. no. 36]. The vigorous young pioneer who would make the land of Israel flourish and provide sustenance for himself and his fellow Jews was the Zionist version of the soldier of other nationalist movements. Such imagery was also intended to combat anti-semitic images of urban Jews as moneylenders and rag dealers by presenting a strong, youthful laborer in touch with nature. This image also incorporates the Magen David (Star of David) which appeared in many forms of Zionist imagery, including pins and banners. At this time, although the Magen David was used as decoration in many synagogues and thus had strong recognition value, it had no strong religious association and could be adapted as a Zionist symbol acceptable to both traditional and non-religious Jews. Figures praying at the Western Wall signify the religious and contemplative life and opportunity to connect to one's Jewish roots afforded by life in Eretz Israel.

Another Zionist theme contrasts the sad plight of Eastern European Jews who required refuge and the help of their Western brethren, with an idealized pastoral landscape representing Eretz Israel, as represented in a souvenir postcard from the Fourth Zionist Congress [cat. no. 42].

Jews of many nations attended the Congress, among them the group from the Caucasus who had their picture taken with Herzl [cat. no. 45] who realized the importance of his own image as a symbol of the Zionist movement. Whatever their nationality, many delegates donned formal dress (including top hats and gloves), as suggested by Herzl, to attend the Congress sessions [cat. no. 39]. This attire blurred differences between delegates, and underlined the occasion's importance. It also emphasized the leaders' perception of the need to present Jewish leaders as financially well-to-do, powerful, serious, established, and worthy of world leaders' respect and attention. A perfect example of the importance of positive presentation, Herzl achieved much by declaring himself the representative of the Jewish people in his efforts to meet with political leaders, and by referring at the First Congress to the achievements of Zionism when very little had been accomplished aside from the convention itself.

Zionist leaders, like those of other national organizations, encouraged the participation of students, as Zionism's link to the future. One autograph letter by Herzl [cat. no. 34] invites Joseph Gedaliah Klausner, age 23, to attend the First Zionist Congress.

Like other contemporary national movements, Zionism had its own flag and rallying songs such as Hatikvah, composed around 1878 by Naftali Herz Imber (1856–1909). Adopted as the Zionist anthem, it expressed traditional yearnings for Zion and helped foster solidarity when sung at meetings. Many copies of the score and lyrics were decorated with Herzl's image [cat. no. 15]. Zionist meetings thus provided a multi-sensory event combining visual stimuli, accompanied by song and occasionally by the consumption of alcohol.[2]

In the footsteps of German nationalists, and of the ethnic-national awakenings of the peoples of Central and Eastern Europe, Zionists viewed language and folkways as important elements of Jewish nature. They realized that a sense of nationhood required tangible dimension, shared national heroes, symbols, songs, and myths, and statehood in a common territory of its own.[3] The Jewish element was provided by Judaism itself, its heritage and culture, and the associations with the ancestral homeland, Eretz Israel. A repertoire of symbols included the Magen David and a visual vocabulary of both programmatic images and images of Zionist leaders. Aditionally, in common with other nationalist movements, Zionism possessed a banner around which they could rally. According to tradition, it was designed by David Wolffsohn and incorporates the stripes of the tallit with the Magen David.

There is another aspect of Zionist imagery which we must consider briefly: its dominance by western European males. While women were involved in the Zionist movement, their numbers represented a small percentage of Congress delegates. The only females with prominent Zionist imagery were Herzl's mother, sister and daughters. Their function is passive; they indicate Victorian family values rather than active feminist issues. Family life was an important component of respectability, even for royalty, in Germany and England. The few women active in the Zionist cause during the early period were made invisible by their exclusion from its imagery. The brave new world order of Zionism, so typical of nationalist stereotypes, centers on young men.

Shtetl Jews are depicted as downtrodden individuals liberated by the efforts of their more fortunate, acculturated Western counterparts, who provided moral and financial support for the good of world Jewry, in the manner of other nationalists.[4] They enabled the *shtetl* Jews to find a secure life as pioneers in Eretz Israel. The visual imagery sometimes depicts this transition as one overseen by Herzl himself [cat. nos. 113 and 150]. Once there, the youth shed their traditional apparel and become young pioneers, while their elders are occasionally viewed at prayer. This served to remind Zionists of the need for strong young men to perform the tasks required for life in Eretz Israel, and visually negated the stereotype of the Jew as a city dweller unable or unwilling to cope with the intensive labor necessary to realize Zionist goals. Zionist imagery is dominated by comfortably circumstanced, successful, Western European bourgeois gentlemen, initially mostly of German background, such as Herzl and Nordau. These men, especially Herzl, laid the foundations of a Jewish national identity centered in Eretz Israel which could provide refuge in times of disaster but need not be one's homeland. It also could be perceived as rendering Zionism respectable as a form of nationalism which did not conflict with allegiance to ones homeland, be it Germany, England or America. Support for Zionism was therefore easily integrated with acculturation and local nationalism [cat. no. 27]. Eastern European Jews and eventually Jews from Eretz Israel as well were increasingly involved in the Zionist movement, and their image incorporated in Zionist iconography, but Herzl's image remained predominant.

Herzl's death from overwork increased the veneration to which he was already subject, but altered the imagery through which it was expressed. His grave became a site of pilgrimage as a manner of experiencing his presence; Zionists no longer able to have their pictures taken beside the great leader, now had their pictures taken beside his grave [cat. no. 17]. Many artifacts were produced which express group and individual mourning. The relationship between Zionism and the German Nationalist youth movements is underscored by a piece of memorial sheet music which refers to Herzl as the Jewish Siegfried and the architect of Zion [cat. no. 15].

Images of heroes and popular figures were traditionally used as personal adornments, both during the hero's life and after death. Mourning jewelry was especially popular during the Victorian period. Images of Herzl in various media were used to decorate watch faces [cat. no. 178], cameos [cat. no. 14] and pins of silver, copper or enameled base metal in memory of this legendary figure and Jewish hero.

One of the best-known memorial images, *Yizkor* [cat. no. 21], was created by artist Boris Schatz. Schatz established the Bezalel School of Arts and Crafts in Jerusalem in 1906 to promote a Hebrew-Jewish artistic style and provide vocational training and jobs for native Jews and new immigrants. But despite the imprimatur of respectability John Ruskin, William Morris and the English Arts and Crafts movement managed to give crafts, most of the Herzl souvenirs did not aspire to that status. Executed in an academic manner, this painting depicts Eastern European Jews mourning Herzl's death in an intensely emotional evocation of mourning. The frame is decorated with motifs popular at the Bezalel School, including the menorah, and with Hebrew lettering of the style developed at the Bezalel School, influenced by Islamic arabesque and European Art Nouveau. *Yizkor* was a popular image, and was also produced as a medal [cat. no. 110] which when sold separately could be hung on the wall; some versions were inserted in the covers of books. Herzl's sanctity and authority were enhanced by what was perceived as his martyrdom in the Zionist cause, and his sacrifice commemorated in such souvenirs.

Just as much of the iconography of this period served as a visual argument against anti-semitic stereotypes, the use of art produced by Jews in a Zionist context contested the stereotype which portrayed Jews as urban intellectuals both unconcerned with and incapable of creative artistic expression. Art exhibitions were held in conjunction with several Congresses. Portraits of important Jewish leaders of the past who advocated a return to Zion decorated the hall of the Basel Casino in which the First Congress met, emphasizing the historical placement of the Zionist movement. An art exhibition was held at the time of the Fifth Zionist Congress which included historical subjects such as Biblical heroes, a visual statement of the shared history of the Jewish people. Martin Buber delivered an address on art at the Fifth Congress, touching on attainments on the path to the revival of Jewish art which would flower once Jews had their own homeland in Eretz Israel. Yet, no one defined Jewish art or the criteria which made a Jewish artist, except perhaps tacitly by permitting their works to be shown in Zionist context.

Herzl was the ideal new type of Jew, the good bourgeois gentleman and man about town, journalist and playwright. His strong physique and handsome appearance conformed to the dominant male stereotype of the period. His appearance countered the stereotype of the Jew as Other, an outsider obviously different from his non-Jewish counterpart. While Herzl's beard enabled more traditional Jews to accept him, his worldliness and sophistication added a dimension to his reputation which commanded respect and admiration of sophisticated Jew and non-Jew alike, and Herzl's meetings with rulers provided social appeal.

Images of Herzl were popular decorations in Jewish homes and the offices of Jewish organizations throughout the world, particularly in Russia and Eastern Europe, where his image joined those of renowned rabbis. Herzl's image adorned calendars, postcards, sheet music, and countless other items. While the predominant iconic image of Herzl shows his left profile, other views have enjoyed popularity. Such images are presented in a variety of media, including decorative textiles [cat. no. 182] and others intended for use [cat. no. 194].

In 1901, Ephraim Moses Lilien (1874–1925) attended the Fifth Zionist Congress in Basel as a delegate; he helped Martin Buber organize the exhibition of Jewish artists to coincide with the Congress, designed a poster for the Congress, and photographed Herzl on the balcony of the *Drei König* Hotel. Lilien, along with Buber and Berthold Feiwel, was one of the founding editors of the *Jüdischer Verlag*, which with Libanon and Phoenix, were the main producers and distributors of Zionist pictures and postcards. He also worked on the Zionist publication *Die Welt* and *Ost und West*, and designed certificates for JNF. Lilien had worked for the German Jugend for several years before becoming associated with Zionism. His illustrations were executed in a manner derived from Art Nouveau or German *Jugendstil*, with its sinuous lines and resemblance to Japanese prints. Several of his illustrations resemble works by Aubrey Beardsley,[5] although Lilien's works are not usually as overtly sexual or decadent as those of Beardsley. A postcard depicting the Creation of Man from *Lieder des Ghetto* (1902), illustrated by Lilien, depicts Herzl as an angel [cat. no. 175]. While it may seem surprising that Lilien depicted Herzl in the nude, this depiction underlines the adherence of Zionist imagery to other contemporary nationalist imagery. The prevailing national male hero was stereotypically pictured in the nude, demonstrating the increasing importance of the outward appearance of male beauty and the influence of Greek heritage on ideals of male beauty.[6] In this context, it is also interesting to note that the Hebrew motto Lilien inscribed on his own *Ex Libris* reads "To the pure all things are pure,"[7] suggesting that Lilien viewed Herzl's person and the cause he represented as being above reproach and able to bear any scrutiny.

A photograph taken by Lilien provided one of the most enduring and popular images of Herzl. It shows the Zionist leader leaning over the balcony of his hotel room in Basel intently regarding something outside the image area to the viewer's left [cat. no. 174]. This image is the perfect expression of yearning and vision. It suggests that Herzl was hopeful, looking towards Eretz Israel and metaphorically seeing Zionist future. After Herzl's demise, images combining Herzl and the land of Israel were constructed relying on this image which was adapted to symbolically place him in Eretz Israel supervising settlement and pioneer efforts [cat. no. 113]. Such images provided a visual metaphor for the intersection of traditional yearning of Jews for a return to Zion, and contemporary, more secular, aspirations. Versions of this Lilien photograph were executed in different media, included JNF stamps and a wall hanging [cat. no. 150]. Formalized by the 1930s, this image of Herzl changed little, perhaps because it possessed an internal, unchanging logic: the hero (Herzl), was always seen at a god-like distance, supervising the welfare of his people.

Images of Herzl executed in micrography, which has been called the only Jewish art form, were popular. This unique decorative feature of Hebrew manuscripts during the late middle ages uses tiny letters to form shapes. Micrographic images of Herzl were usually composed of the text of *Der Judenstaat* [cat. no. 172] or *Altneuland*.

Countless souvenirs and decorative objects depicting Herzl were produced in Israel both before and after it became a state. Busts of famous individuals were among the popular bibelots with which people decorated their homes to display their commitment to aesthetics as well as political and social causes. The materials were inexpensive—paper, wood, metal and plaster, and mass-production kept these pieces affordable by a majority of Zionists. Other tourist trade items, including plaques and pipe rests were made of olive wood, evokings Eretz Israel at a reasonable price.

Initially, Herzl's image was preeminent among Zionist subjects, or placed in the company of prominent philanthropists such as Sir Moses Montefiore, and political figures. A scrap [cat. no. 28] depicts Herzl, Mandelstamm and Nordau with a Magen David (Star of David). It also depicts scenes juxtaposing people praying at the Western Wall and a man sowing in a field. Scraps, popular during the Victorian period were sometimes pasted in albums or used to decorate greeting cards.

An unusual image of Herzl decorates the cover of a Haggadah [cat. no. 32]. Here, Herzl welcomes Lord Balfour to heaven after the latter's death. Lord Arthur James Balfour (1848–1930) was British foreign secretary, and wrote the historic declaration to Lord Rothschild on November

2, 1917, pledging British support for a Jewish national home in Palestine. The artwork perfectly demonstrates the ease with which new historical events could be framed within the established iconography.

More commonly, the images of popular contemporary heroes were merely juxtaposed with that of Herzl. One piece in the Anson collection depicts Herzl with Golda Meir, Moshe Dayan and others, demonstrating that Herzl's image remained popular as the founder of the State of Israel [cat. no. 33].

Herzl memorabilia have been executed in many styles over time; even the Bezalel School produced works in different contemporary and traditional styles. Three works in the Anson collection made at the Bezalel School are decorated in diverse manners. One, a plaque on a wooden mount [cat. no. 147], is simple; the bosses by which the plaque is attached to the wooden backing are incorporated into the design in the manner of international manifestations of the Arts and Crafts movement. A dish [cat. no. 148] is executed in damascene, brass inlaid with copper and silver, a style with local connotations. Another plaque designed by Boris Schatz, uses the sinuous curves of Art Nouveau [cat. no. 146]. This plaque equates Herzl with Moses, who led the Jewish people to the Promised Land but did not live to see the culmination of his dream. At the same time, it mythologizes Herzl as the leader of his people and the contemporary Moses.

In 1948, David Ben Gurion proclaimed the foundation of the State of Israel while standing under an image of Theodor Herzl [cat. no. 82]. This serves as a visual reminder of the long period of struggle from the publication of *Der Judenstaat* to that historic moment, and the perception of debt to Herzl. Interestingly, a color postcard depicting Ben Gurion's proclamation is also a record which plays *Hatikvah*. The reburial of Herzl following the creation of the State of Israel further underlined Herzl's heroic status in Jewish history.

In his will, Herzl mentioned that he wanted to be buried in a metal coffin, so that his remains could be transferred to the State of Israel. His vision was realized in 1949 when, with great ceremony, his coffin was taken from Vienna to what is now Mount Herzl in Israel. Herzl's image was thus woven into the political fabric of the State of Israel, confirming the achievement of Zionism; at the same time, the reinterment was a symbolic empowerment of the government of Israel as the successor of Herzl, a celebration of the continuity between Zionist past and present, and the power of faith. In a sense the State was drawing on Herzl's mystique and the power of his image, as well as paying homage to the man who laid the groundwork which lead to the foundation of the State. The pageantry of the reburial is represented in the Anson collection by photographs of the casket being carried by an honor guard, and by a pin identifying a member of the honor guard [cat. no. 79].

Memorials to Herzl took many forms. Lectures were held on the anniversary of his demise, organizations were named for him [cat. no. 19], streets were named in his honor, as was an early ship in the Zim line. [cat. no. 93].

The mechanics of establishing a national homeland prompted the creation of a bank and a fund-raising organization which also relied on visual imagery. The Jewish Colonial Trust was incorporated in 1899 to promote the development and immigration of Jews to Eretz Israel. It handled financial transactions relating to immigration and to development within Eretz Israel. The funds share certificates reproduced the juxtaposition of the young pioneer and prayer at the Western Wall [cat. no. 61] familiar from earlier Zionist iconography.

Supplies of postage stamps often ran out during the Israeli War of Independence, and stamps had to be improvised, among them Jewish National Fund labels with Herzl's image. [cat. no. 83] During the first year of the State, Herzl's image was used on souvenir Israeli postal envelopes four times, and several stamps have been issued with his image.

Zionist Congresses have met since 1897. From the First Congress, Herzl realized the importance of these meetings which advertised the Zionist cause in a very public manner. These congresses generated a vast amount of memorabilia, including postcards, delegates' and visitors' cards. While many of the postcards depicted views of the city in which the conference was held, others were specially designed by artists. Delegates to the Congresses wore badges which took many forms over the years. The Convention Hall, built in Jerusalem in 1951 to house meetings of the Zionist Congresses, was a potent symbol of the success and continuation of Zionism.

The nineteenth century saw a dramatic increase in the number of medals created, many with Jewish subjects. These included portraits of notable contemporary Jews, and images of synagogues and charitable institutions struck to commemorate their opening or anniversaries. Medals with Zionist themes often incorporate the image of Herzl, usually in profile, either alone or in the company of contemporary Zionist figures, or Herzl's statement "It is no dream." The first important Zionist medal was made by Samuel Friedrich Beer (1846–1912) to commemorate the Second Zionist Congress [cat. no. 106]. On the obverse, is an image of a female figure in antique garment. The number of medals increased with the creation of the State of Israel. Several mark anniversaries of its creation, others commemorate important events in its history such as the Entebbe victory and the liberation of Jerusalem. Herzl's image also appeared on Israeli currency—the 100 lirah bill of 1973 and 10 shekel coins of 1984 [cat. no. 143].

Many pendants, stick pins and other forms of wearable medals have been struck with Herzl's image for Zionist youth organizations or conventions, or distributed as prizes for students. Stick pins [cat. no. 112] predominate among the earlier pieces. An acceptable form of masculine jewelry and therefore suitable for Congress delegates, stick pins could also be used by women. Several of these objects take the form of the Magen David; one frames Herzl's face with a blue and white enamel Magen David [cat. no. 108]; another frames the image of the Second Congress medal [cat. no. 109].

At each period, souvenirs of different types and styles have been produced. A selection of items from the Anson collection produced since 1960 demonstrates current consumer interests. Recent items include: chocolates with a raised image of Herzl [cat. no. 205], T-shirts, shopping bags, telephone cards [cat. no. 208] and colored versions of the traditional images of Herzl's life including the balcony pose in postcards. In common with earlier items, these souvenirs are tangible expressions of the owner's excitement at the existence of the State of Israel, and an outlet through which the owner can vicariously participate in an exciting period in history. But they also represent a recognition of the commercial value of Herzl's image in addition to its value as a Zionist, nationalist symbol. The recent proliferation of new artifacts celebrating the centennial of *Der Judenstaat* and of the First Zionist Congress demonstrates the continuing cultural investment in the Herzl mythology.

In the capitalist societies of Europe and America, the catchy design of souvenirs, the opportunity to share the sense of belonging to the group and to the commemoration of a hero, attracted buyers for products without regard to a need for the item. The images of Jews praying at the Western Wall; agricultural scenes; the Magen David (Star of David); and depictions of Herzl continued to function as a form of self expression and group consciousness among world Jewry. Herzl's image as a symbolic expression of group solidarity and goals retains its psychological power to the present day. The early Zionist iconographic construction of Herzl continues to shape our perception of Herzl, the Zionist movement, and the creation of the State.

This exhibition enables us to see early Zionist iconography as a complex cultural creation which enjoyed great success. Yet, it was fraught with tensions which we can perceive clearly from our vantage point in the second half of the twentieth century. Its imagery manipulates the viewer to focus on a specific set of values and a shared view of origins and purpose, thus promoting a sense of solidarity among world Zionists. In Eretz Israel, the natural Jewish homeland, Jews from many nations would meld into a new Jew, the healthy young Zionist, whose labors would better his personal circumstances, change the world insofar as both non-Jews' perception of Jews, and re-establish the Jewish homeland. Zionist imagery made this change from impoverished wanderer fleeing persecution to vigorous pioneer in an ideal land appear simple and natural, while in reality, immigration to a new country, accomodation to a new way of life, and forging a new cultural identity are all aspects of a complex process. The iconography is clearly gendered, giving primacy to the male experience, both in the Zionist organizations and in Eretz Israel. Its prominent actors are western Europeans, who act on behalf of their less fortunate eastern brothers. The role of women during the early Zionist period is marginalized, as is the place of the observant Jew in Eretz Israel. While religion is occasionally acknowledged as a component of Zionist life, it is visually downplayed as a role primarily allocated to the elderly, or it is ignored altogether.

The popularity of Herzl's phrase, "If you will it, it is not a dream," can be understood on several levels. Its formulation by Herzl reveals his ability as a writer, and his awareness of the power of understatement and condensation of meaning to evoke complex concepts. In common with secular and religious mottoes popular in Victorian culture, it was short and easily remembered, easy to fit on a variety of media (coinage, postcards, dishes etc.). The values and beliefs underlying the use of this quotation in Zionist context make it a popular decorative motif, alone or, more commonly, in conjunction with an image of Herzl himself. As an expression of the Zionist goal, it testifies to the powerful continuing cultural force of Zionism from its earliest usage as an expression of hope for the future, to the present day when it expresses the enduring fundamental Zionist achievement, the existence of the State of Israel.

This investigation of Herzl as Zionist a cult figure, both icon and subject of certain rituals such as visits to his tomb and office, relies on the investigation of mundane artifacts, a category which Herzl himself integrated into the Zionist vocabulary in the form of Congress postcards and other ephemeral souvenirs. It demonstrates that such artifacts were used to convey both simple and complex metaphorical concepts about culture and identity, about Herzl's role as Zionist hero and a hero of the State of Israel, and to convey a range of Zionist and nationalist ideals. The discourse articulated by this imagery remains both meaningful and powerful to the present day.

Bonni-Dara Michaels, Yeshiva University Museum Registrar/Curator, served as exhibition curator of "Theodor Herzl: If you will it, it is not a dream."

FOOTNOTES

1. I would like to thank Manfred and Judy Anson for making me welcome during the weeks spent cataloging, and Joel and Debby Anson for their kindness during that period when I must have always seemed underfoot. I am indebted to all the members of the YUM team who helped make this exhibition and catalog a success. Special thanks to: Director Sylvia Herskowitz, a wonderful inspiration and editor, without whose vision this exhibition would not have come about; Curator Gabriel Goldstein who kindly answered questions, helped with Hebrew, and assited as editor; and Assistant Joelle Bollag and docent volunteer Rosette Pascal who helped catalog the Anson collection at the cost of sore hands and dusty knees.

2. Michael Berkowitz, *Zionist Culture and West European Jewry before the First World War.* Cambridge: Cambridge University Press, 1993, p. 20.

3. *ibid.,* p. 41.

4. George Mosse, *Nationalism and Sexuality: Respectability and Abnormal Sexuality in Modern Europe.* New York: Howard Fertig, 1985, p. 78.

5. Milly Heyd, "Lillien and Beardsley: to the pure all things are pure," *Journal of Jewish Art* 7(1980): 58–69.

6. George Mosse, *op. cit.,* p. 76.

7. Milly Heyd, *op. cit.,* p. 58.

SELECTED BIBLIOGRAPHY

Berkowitz, Michael, "Art in Zionist Popular Culture and Jewish National Self-Consciousness, 1897–1914," *Art and Its Uses: The Visual Image and Modern Jewish Society, Studies in Contemporary Jewry* 6 (1990) 9–42.

———. *Zionist Culture and West European Jewry before the First World War.* Cambridge: Cambridge University Press, 1993.

Bertram, Fred. *Epic in Sculpture: The Medallic History of the Jewish People*, conceived and Directed by Robert Weber. New York: The Judaic Heritage Society, 1974.

Felton, Anton. *Jewish Carpets: A History and Guide.* England: Antique Collectors' Club, 1997.

Haffner, Sylvia. *Israel's Modern Money and Medals 1917–1970.* 1967. Tarzana, California: Philip J. Matthew, 1970.

Kornberg, Jacques. "Theodor Herzl: A Reevaluation," *Journal of Modern History*, 52 (June 1980), 226–52.

Loewenberg, Peter. "Theodor Herzl: A Psychoanalytic Study in Charismatic Leadership," In *The Psychoanalytic Interpretation of History*, edited by Benjamin B. Wolman, pp. 150–91. New York: Basic Books, 1971.

Mosse, George. *Nationalism and Sexuality: Respectability and Abnormal Sexuality in Modern Europe.* New York: Howard Fertig, 1985.

Narkiss, M. "The Arts Portray Herzl." In *Theodore Herzl: A Memorial.* Edited by Meyer Weisgal, pp. 119–120. New York: New Palestine, 1929.

Tel Aviv, Bet Hatefutsot. *Kahol Ve-Levan be-Zevaim.* Rahel Arbel, ed. 1996.

Tel Aviv, Tel Aviv Museum. *Herzl in Profile: Herzl's Image in the Applied Arts.* David Tartakover, ed. 1978–79.

Vienna, Jewish Museum of the City of Vienna. *Judenfragen: Jewish Attitudes from Assimilation to Zionism.* Exhibition 25 October 1996 to 16 February 1997.

Vital, David, *The Origins of Zionism.* Oxford: Oxford University Press, 1975.

DER JUDENSTAAT, FIRST EDITION, AUTOGRAPHED BY HERZL. CAT. NO. 2

Exhibition Checklist

The following checklist consists of selections from the more than 450 artifacts from the Anson collection displayed at Yeshiva University Museum. All artifacts here described are from the Anson collection, unless otherwise specified. Our selection criteria for inclusion in this catalogue include the artifact's significance and our ability to provide attribution information. The checklist primarily follows the order of the exhibition. Individual works are listed in chronological order in each section. Works by known artists are listed by artist; where the artist is unknown, they are listed by title. All measurements are in inches, height preceding width. No measurements are given for books or for late 20th century periodicals. All Biblical quotations are cited in English as they appear on the artifact; where no English is inscribed, the translation follows the 1985 edition of the Jewish Publication Society.

During Herzl's Lifetime

Rapid strides in photography in the late 19th century made possible the documentation of Herzl's social and political life and his work for the Zionist cause. Portraits of Herzl, his activities and family were reproduced in postcards and books, and copied in other media.

Herzl began a journalistic career in Vienna, serving on the staff of the liberal *Neue Freie Presse*, reporting mainly on his impressions and observations of various European cities. As a correspondent, he was present at the Dreyfus trial in Paris which made a strong and lasting impression on this sophisticated assimilated Jew.

The Anson collection provides an opportunity to examine Herzl's social and political life in the form of original publications and photographs reproduced in postcard form. Such postcards are but one of many easily accessible artifacts of material culture which demonstrate the continuing centrality of Herzl to the identity of world Zionism.

1. Das Palais Bourbon: Bilder aus dem französischen Parlamentsleben
(The Palais Bourbon: Pictures of the Parliamentary Life of France)

Theodor Herzl
Dunder & Humbolt
Leipzig, 1895
9 x 5 3/4 x 1/2 in.

Articles in which Herzl investigated the proceedings and character of parliamentarians, originally written for the *Neue Freie Presse*, are gathered in this publication.

2. Der Judenstaat: Versuch einer Modernen Lösung der Judenfrage
(The Jewish State: An Attempt at a Modern Solution to the Jewish Question)

Theodor Herzl
Autograph first edition
Leipzig and Vienna: M. Breitenstein's Verlags-Buchandlung, 1896
9 1/2 x 6 1/2 in.

This is an autographed copy of the first edition of Herzl's seminal publication. (illus. on p. 50)

3. A Jewish State: An attempt at a Modern Solution of the Jewish Question

Theodor Herzl
Translated by H. Sylvie d'Avigdor
First English translation
London: David Nutt, 1896
8 3/4 x 5 3/4 in.

Der Judenstaat was so popular that it was translated into five languages, including English, French and Russian, in the first year after its initial publication.

4. Das Neue Ghetto (The New Ghetto)

Theodor Herzl
Warsaw, 1898
8 x 5 1/2 in.

Herzl hoped that this play would bring the Jewish question to a more broad public awareness, thus encouraging open discussion of the issue, which hitherto was discussed in more private surroundings, and reciprocal tolerance between Jews and Christians.

5. Solon in Lydia: Schauspiel in drei Akten (Solon in Lydia: Spectacle in Three Acts)

Theodor Herzl
Wiener Verlag
Vienna and Leipzig, 1904
7 1/2 x 6 3/4 in.

In this play, Herzl portrays the Athenian lawgiver, Solon, as advisor at the court of King Croesus of Lydia (d. ca. 546 B.C.E.).

6. Postcard: Herzls Mutter, Jeannette Herzl (Herzl's Mother: Jeannette Herzl)

Photograph.– Kunstlerkarte 3001. Ser.p.7
Jüdischer Nationalfonds, Betar
Palästina–1912–H.L.i.W.–
Inscription dated 1916
5 3/4 x 3 3/4 in.

Herzl's mother, born Jeannette Diamant, supported her son in his Zionist endeavors and was his frequent companion. This image presents her in her later years, stylishly dressed in mourning for her son. The popularity of images of Herzl's mother underlines the desire of Zionists to envision their hero in the role of a good son.

7. Postcard: Theodor Herzl in seinem Arbeitszimmer (Theodor Herzl in his office)

Postmark Vienna, Austria, April 21, 1937
5 3/4 x 3 3/4 in.

Images of Herzl and members of his family were popular Zionist images. Here, Herzl is depicted with his three children in his study in Vienna. This image focuses attention on several characteristics of Herzl as a cultured European intellectual gentleman, an author, and a good family man. Close examination of the image reveals a rather stiff Herzl, despite the relaxed embrace of one of his daughters.

8. Postcard: Pauline Herzl im 8 Lebensjahr (Pauline Herzl at Age Eight)

Postmark Vienna 14 Mai 1937
4 3/4 x 3 in.

Herzl had a very close relationship with his older sister, Pauline, who died young in 1878.

9. Postcard: Theodor Herzls Kinder im Jahre 1897 (Theodor Herzl's Children in 1897)

Postmark Vienna, Austria, April 20, 1938
6 x 3 3/4 in.

Images of Herzl's children were popular Zionist souvenirs. The postmark on this example includes the words "Des Führers Geburtstag" (The Leader's birthday), indicating that Zionist souvenirs continued to be purchased and mailed despite the Nazi regime. It also brings to mind the fact that Herzl's youngest daughter, Margarethe (Trude), died in Theresienstadt in 1943.

CAT. NO. 7

POSTCARD: VISITORS NEXT TO HERZL'S TOMBSTONE, VIENNA, EARLY 20TH CENTURY. CAT. NO. 17

Herzl's Death Memorialized

Tragically, Herzl died at age 44 of a heart condition and pneumonia. In his will, he requested that he be interred in Israel when statehood was achieved. He strengthened his own legend by thus demonstrating his faith in the eventual triumph of Zionism and the creation of a Jewish state.

Already almost a legend during his lifetime, his renown crescendoed after his untimely death. Zionist publications summarized his life and works, using traditional images of Herzl and his family, and new images were added to the repertoire. Postcards and photographs were published depicting Herzl's grave in Vienna, and commemorating visits to the tomb by members of various Zionist organizations. Such visits, and the purchase and display of postcards and other artifacts depicting Herzl, were visible manifestations of identification with the Zionist movement. Though Herzl could no longer be depicted as a participant in Zionist functions and at Congresses, his image was incorporated as if he were approving and guiding contemporary Zionist endeavors.

After his untimely death, Herzl's name was bestowed on streets and organizations, and the anniversary of his death provided the occasion for memorial meetings of Zionist organizations around the world. After the establishment of the State of Israel, the Zim Line even named a ship for Herzl. Thus, Zionist organizations and the State of Israel itself demonstrated, by their continued use of the Herzl as icon, their continued investment in the myth of Herzl the Hero, pre-eminent founder of Zionism,without whom there would have been no State of Israel.

10. *Jüdische Rundschau*
Organ der Zionistischen Vereinigung für
Deutschland (Jewish Panorama; Organ of the
Zionist Association for Germany)
Sonderausgabe zum Andeken an Theodor Herzl
(Special edition in Memory of Theodor Herzl)

Berlin, 1904
9 1/2 x 6 1/2 in.

Zionist organizations in different countries published their own journals. This is one of the special editions published in Herzl's memory.

11. *Die Welt (The World)*
"The Death of Theodor Herzl"

Number 29
Vienna, 15 July 1904
12 x 9 1/4 in.

Begun by Herzl himself, this journal became the official organ of the Zionist organization.

12. *Ost und West*
(East and West)

Herzl Memorial Volume
Berlin, 1904
11 1/2 x 8 1/2 in.

Ost und West was a Zionist publication of the Juedischer Verlag, published from 1901 to 1922.

13. *Postcard: VII Zionist Congress*
27 Juli – 6 August 1905
[Hebrew and English]

Hebrew inscription:
"...and you shall carry up my bones from here with you" (Exodus 13:19)
Artist: Carl Pollak
Handwritten German inscriptions:
Vom Kongress ohne Herzl senden viele Grüsse Eduard [signed] Joseph Schwarz; Hoffentlich habt ihr meine brochure in... (Eduard, Best wishes from the Congress without Herzl, Joseph

Schwarz; hopefully you have read my
brochure…)
Postmark Basel 26 July 1905
3 1/2 x 5 1/2 in.

Eight years before he designed this image, Carl
Pollak designed the postcards, delegates' and visitors' cards for the First Zionist Congress. At that
time, he was a university student who worked in
the Zionist office in Vienna.

Herzl's image remained important, signifying
Zionism and identification with the Zionist cause.
Here he regards a group of men bearing a Zionist
banner with seven five-pointed stars representing
the seven-hour work day envisioned by Herzl.

At this time, the only item that could be written on one side of the postcard was the recipient's
name and address, hence the salutations were
written around the image.

Cameos had long been in vogue among the
wealthy due to interest in Greek and Roman art
and archaeology and revivals of classical forms in
art; when this pin was produced, cameos were
widely available in a variety of price ranges.

Right profile images of Herzl such as this one
are more rare than views of his left profile. The
artist who produced the cameo carved the beard
in long twisted curls reminiscent of those of
Michelangelo's figure of Moses, in marked contrast
to the tight curls of the hair on Herzl's head.

15. Sheet Music:
Dr. Herzl Elegy; Funeral Meditations on the
Death of the Jewish Siegfried Zion's Architect

Composed and Arranged by
Prof. Herman S. Shapiro
Words by Prof. G. Selikowitz
Published and copyright H.S. Shapiro
New York, early 20th century
14 x 11 1/8 in.

The imagery on the cover of this memorial song
sheet is fairly standard for the period. It incorporates an image of Herzl surrounded by a classical
wreath signifying triumph and heroism. Herzl is
referred to as the Jewish Siegfried, the legendary
hero of the German nationalist movement.
(illus. on p. 22)

CAT. NO. 14

14. Cameo Pin With Portrait of Theodor Herzl

Hebrew inscription (reverse): Herzl
Early 20th century
Shell; jet(?)
2 3/4 x 2 1/4 in.

While commemorative jewelry honoring the dead
had been popular for centuries, it became quite
fashionable during the Victorian period, influenced in part by the intense mourning of Queen
Victoria. Black substances including jet (a dense
form of coal) were employed in the creation of
mourning jewelry.

CAT. NO. 13

16. Pop-up New Year's Greeting Card with view of the Herzl Gymnasium

Yiddish inscription: Panorama of Tel Aviv
Germany, ca. 1910
10 1/4 x 9 3/4 in.

The Herzl Gymnasium was an important feature of the Tel-Aviv skyline during the early part of this century. This three-dimensional New Year's card juxtaposes a woman holding a Zionist banner against the backdrop of Tel-Aviv.

17. Postcard: Visitors Posing Next to Herzl's Tombstone

Hebrew inscription: Tomb of Herzl in Vienna
Early 20th century
5 1/2 x 3 1/2 in.

Many Jews made the pilgrimage to Herzl's tomb in Vienna as a gesture of respect for their fallen hero, just as they traditionally visited the graves of venerated rabbis. A photograph documenting their visit was a common souvenir. Here five young men stare solemnly at the camera, as was the custom at the time when having one's photograph taken; the banner of their organization folded beside them. (illus. on p. 54)

18. Postcard: Tel-Aviv, The Gymnasium

Eretz Israel, early 20th century
3 3/4 x 5 1/2 in.

Many institutions and organizations were named for Herzl, including the secondary school in Tel-Aviv, known variously as the Gymnasia Herzlia and the Herzl Gymnasium, which prepared students for university. Founded in 1906, it was a symbol of Zionist achievement in Eretz Israel and of the unique Jewish education it provided.

19. Membership Ribbon

DR. THEODOR HERZEL (sic)
Lodge No. 183
I.O.B.A.
INDEPENDENT ORDER
BRITH ABRAHAM
PHILA.

Pennsylvania, first half of 20th century
Fabric: metal, enamel; Fringe: gilt metal strips wrapped around thread core
8 x 2 7/8 in.

An offshoot of Brith Abraham, the Independent Order of Brith Abraham was established in 1887. A fraternal order, it provided medical assitance to members, helped them become citizens, and provided various forms of support in times of bereavement. Reaching its peak membership in the 1930s, it was the largest Jewish fraternal order in the world.

20. Notice of a Herzl Memorial Meeting

Congregation Zedeck
Burlington, Vermont, 1920
12 x 9 in.

21. Yizkor

Boris Schatz (1867–1932)
Hebrew inscription: *Kel Maleh Rahamim*...the prince and great in Israel Binyamin Zeev son of Yaakov known as Theodor Herzl, may his memory be for a blessing. May he rest in the Garden of Eden...Amen. Born in Budapest the 10th of the month of Iyar died in Erlach the 20th of the month of Tammuz.

Oil on panel
Early 20th century
Frame: copper, repoussé, painted
30 x 53 in. panel; 45 x 73 in. framed
Yeshiva University Museum 88.19
Gift of Jewish Community Center of Greater Baltimore

Boris Schatz, founder of the Bezalel School of Arts and Crafts in Jerusalem, used the academic style

to convey the spiritual aspect in this depiction of men mourning Herzl's death. The frame is typical of Bezalel, decorated with popular motifs including the menorah and symbols of the Twelve Tribes. The inscription is executed in Hebrew lettering of the style developed at the Bezalel School, influenced by Islamic arabesque and European Art Nouveau.

The Bezalel school held exhibitions in various cities in Europe and America, sometimes in conjunction with meetings of the Zionist Congress where works like this one by Schatz would be displayed. The sale of these works helped support the Bezalel school.

22. Notice of a Memorial Meeting In Tribute to the Memory of Dr. Theodor Herzl

Temple Mishkan Tefila Schoolhouse
Roxbury, Massachusetts, 1940
13 3/8 x 8 1/2 in.

Memorial meetings in Herzl's honor continued to be held by synagogues and Zionist organizations long after his death.

23. Postcard: Sketch Depicting Herzl's Original Tombstone

Artist: Samuel Kretschmer (1894-1972)
Hebrew inscription: Dr. Binyamin Zeev Herzl
born 5 Iyar 1860 died 2 Tammuz 1904
Keren Kajemeth le'Jisrael (Jüd. Nationalfonds)
Vienna, before 1949
5 3/4 x 3 1/2 in.

Kretschmer's depiction of Herzl's tomb in Vienna is typical of mourning imagery, combining as it does an image of the deceased with tombstone and memorial flames. He has, however, idealized the surroundings of the grave. (illus. on p. 36)

24. Postcard: SS. Theodor Herzl [Hebrew and English]

Zim Navigation Co. Ltd.
Israel; postmark 28.5.57
3 3/4 x 5 1/2 in.

One of the ships of Israel's Zim line was named for Herzl. The ship and its interior were depicted in color and black and white on souvenir postcards.

Herzl and Other Notables

A pantheon of figures headed by Theodor Herzl comprised the secular hagiography of Zionist imagery, most commonly encountered in the form of artifacts of popular culture, primarily postcards. It was through this medium that Zionism found visual expression, and that Zionist issues and the features of Zionist leaders reached their largest audience.

Initially, Herzl's image was preeminent among Zionist subjects, or placed in the company of prominent philanthropists such as Sir Moses Montefiore, or other political figures. A scrap depicts Herzl, Mandelstamm and Nordau with a Magen David (Star of David) and scenes drawn from Zionist iconography depicting people praying at the Western Wall and a man sowing in a field. This is an allusion both to the Biblical Land of Israel and to the development of agricultural settlements in the Homeland. Scraps were popular during the Victorian period; often they were collected in albums, or used to decorate screens and greeting cards.

In 1930, the death of Lord Balfour, architect of the Balfour Declaration' occasioned the production of a Haggadah, the cover of which depicts Herzl welcoming him to Paradise (the Garden of Eden).

As new heroes arrived on the scene, their images were juxtaposed with that of Herzl. One image shows him with Golda Meir, Moshe Dayan and others, demonstrating that Herzl's image remained popular as the founder of the State of Israel, in whose footsteps the current leaders of Israel follow.

25. Postcard Depicting Zionist Leaders: Lazare, Mandelstamm, Gaster, Nordau, Herzl

Hebrew inscription: "...I am going to take the Israelite people from among the nations...and bring them to their own land." (Ezekiel 37.21); Second Congress
Ca. 1898
5 1/2 x 3 1/2 in.

The Second Zionist Congress met in Basel August 28–31, 1898. The decoration on this card consists of the images of secular and religious Zionist leaders; the Magen David (Star of David) which had become a Zionist symbol; an image of a young pioneer farming in Eretz Israel; and figures praying at the Western Wall. The combination of religious and secular imagery provides visual support for Zionism representing a unified Jewry. This theme is repeated in the depictions of Eretz Israel as a place where work and prayer both have a place. The lower half of this image was later printed separately by Hebrew Publishing Company (cat. no. 28).

CAT. NO. 25

26. Postcard Depicting: Herzl, Nordau and Printz(?)

Inscribed: Prosit Neujahr! Angenohme Feiertage. Herzliche Grüsse. Hempler (New Year's Cheers! Pleasant Holidays. Best Regards.)
Postmarks Prague and Vienna, 1899
3 3/4 x 5 1/2 in.

This card juxtaposes images of Zionist leaders and a Magen David (Star of David) with a scene of young men fencing. Fencing organizations were popular in Europe at the time; Theodor Herzl was a member of one for a brief time while at the University of Vienna. He resigned in response to a rising tide of anti-semitism.

27. Postcard Depicting Zionist leaders: Sokolow, Birnbaum, Nordau, Ussishkin, Herzl, Zangwill, and Wolffsohn

Inscription: A Happy New Year
Hebrew Publishing Co., No.64
Early 20th century
3 1/2 x 5 1/2 in.

Printed greeting cards were still a relatively new phenomenon at the time that this New Year's card was produced for the American consumer market. It combines images of the heroes and symbols of Zionism with an American flag. It serves as a visual structuring of Zionism as capable of co-existing with American patriotism.

CAT. NO. 27

CAT. NO. 28

28. Scrap with Zionist Figures [Herzl, Nordau, Mandelstamm] and Motifs

Hebrew inscription: "…I am going to take the Israelite people from among the nations…and bring them to their own land." (Ezekiel 37.21)
Hebrew Publishing Co.
New York, 1909
Chromolithograph
3 1/4 x 3 1/4 in.

During the Victorian period, small paper images known as scraps were used much the same way in which stickers are used today. They were collected in albums, or pasted on paper, special boxes or screens.

This is one of a number of scraps with Zionist motifs. Here, Herzl is framed by a Magen David (Star of David) between two other Zionist leaders. Below them are scenes of life in Eretz Israel: a farmer sowing seed, and figures praying at the Western Wall. The Hebrew inscription stresses the traditional Jewish hope for a return to Zion.

Although scraps were available from the early 1800s, production methods improved later in the century. Steel plates were substituted for lithographic stones, and the use of belt-driven steam powered presses made the mass production of scraps faster and cheaper.

29. Album: A Happy New Year

Keller's Map of Palestine, Jerusalem and Syria
Hebrew Publishing Company
E.C. Bridgman, lithographers
New York, 1910
Book 4 1/2 x 5 1/2 in.; map 23 1/2 x 19 3/4 in.

Prominent Jewish figures, scenes of Israel, and episodes from Herzl's life are all depicted on the reverse of a map of Eretz Israel issued as a New Year's gift. These images forge a visual connection between the heroes of Zionism and their territorial goal.

30. Postcard Depicting Herzl and Nordau
A Happy New Year

Hebrew Publishing Co.
Series 5 #26
New York, Postmark September 5, 1920
3 3/4 x 5 1/2 in.

Max Nordau, a physician and scientist, was one of the great Zionist theoreticians and author of such popular texts as *Conventional Lies of Our Civilization* (1883). Like Herzl, his physical appearance, evoked Biblical prophets.

31. Postcard Depicting Wolffsohn and Herzl

Publisher: Central, #1579
Printed in Germany, early 20th century
3 3/4 x 5 1/2 in.

David Wolffsohn (1856–1914) received a traditional Jewish education in his native Lithuania.

CAT. NO. 31

After holding several different jobs, he managed to prosper in the timber business. He met Herzl in 1896, and eventually became the second president of the World Zionist Organization.

This was one of a series of Zionist cards pairing Zionist leaders. Another from the series (#1576) in the Anson Collection depicts Nordau rather than Wolffsohn at left. The motifs at the bottom center of the card suggest general literary and artistic accomplishments and do not refer to Zionism.

CAT. NO. 32

32. Haggadah for the National Home [Hebrew]

Zeev Navon
Publisher: "Red Sea"
Printer: Atin and Shoshani
Tel Aviv, 1930
9 1/4 x 6 1/4 in.

The cover of this Haggadah is decorated with a sketch of Theodor Herzl as an angel, welcoming Lord Arthur James Balfour (1848–1930) to Paradise. As British foreign secretary, Balfour wrote the historic declaration to Lord Rothschild on November 2, 1917, pledging British support for a Jewish national home in Palestine. The artwork on this cover demonstrates the ease with which established iconography was structured to convey a Zionist message.

33. Postcard depicting Herzl, Meir, Dayan, Shaskar, Lescoff

Designed by: Arieh Moskowitz
Israel, 1971
5 1/2 x 4 in.

This postcard, designed for Israeli Independence Day, celebrates recent Israeli political and military accomplishments and heroes, visually locating them in the historical Zionist success story by juxtaposing the contemporary figures and shield of the State of Israel with an image of Theodor Herzl. It is interesting to note that, just as the different shape of a halo (round or square) on traditional icons served to differentiate the figures represented, so the image of Herzl is placed within a Magen David (Star of David) while the features of living heroes are placed within a circle.

CAT. NO. 33

Zionist Congress

Herzl orchestrated and chaired the First Zionist Congress, held in Basel in 1897. This Congress brought together Jewish representatives from around the world. From the time of the First Congress, Herzl realized the importance of these meetings in promoting the Zionist cause in a very public manner. The Congresses generated and continue to generate a vast amount of memorabilia, including postcards, delegates' and visitors' cards, which constitute the primary manner in which the majority of members experience the organization. Delegates to the Congresses are issued badges which have taken many forms over the years. Among these is the shekel form of the 23rd Congress of 1951, the first to be held in Israel.

Art and culture were important issues at the Congresses. An exhibition of paintings was held in conjunction with the Fifth Congress in 1901. Lesser Ury, one of the artists whose works were included in this exhibition, later designed a postcard for the 12th Congress. While some postcards were specially designed for Congresses, others depict views of the cities in which the Congresses were held. In 1951, a Convention Hall was built in Jerusalem to house meetings of the Zionist Congress, a potent symbol of the importance and continuation of Zionism.

34. Handwritten Letter inviting Joseph Gedaliah Klausner (1874–1958) to attend the First Zionist Congress

Theodor Herzl
July 29, 1897
7 1/2 x 4 1/2 in.; Framed 8 x 10 1/4 in.

Although most of the primary material dealing with Herzl's life is in the Central Zionist Archives in Jerusalem, one occasionally finds autograph letters in private hands.

In 1897, Klausner was studying Semitic and modern languages at Heidelberg, Germany. He was a proponent of the revival of Hebrew as a spoken language, an important element in the contemporary awakening of national Jewish consciousness.

Like all leaders of nationalist movements, Zionist leaders realized that students represented the future of their cause, and they actively encouraged students to participate. This personal letter from Herzl inspired the young Klausner to attend the First Zionist Congress in Basel, and he continued to remain an active Zionist throughout his life.

35. Postcard: Group portrait of delegates to the First Zionist Congress

A Happy New Year (Hebrew and English)
Hebrew Publishing Co. #49
New York, early 20th century
3 1/2 x 5 1/2 in.

A composite image consisting of the faces of all delegates to the First Zionist Congress enjoyed great popularity. Herzl's image, larger than those of the other participants, was at the center of the group. This New Year's greeting reproduces a section of the larger composition.

36. Postcard: II ZIONISTEN-CONGRESS in Basel (II Zionist Congress in Basel)

Artist: Menahem Okin
Hebrew inscription: "I am going to take the Israelite people from among the nations...and bring them to their own land."
(Ezekiel 37.21)
Basel, 1898
3 1/2 x 5 1/2 in.

Official postcards from the Zionist Congresses like this one were among the earliest Zionist products available to the general public. It incorporates several of the main Zionist motifs. The Magen David (Star of David) was familiar to many people from contemporary synagogues, and was used on philanthropic and community seals. The young man farming an idyllic landscape against the rising sun was a Zionist icon, in contrast to the armed soldiers of other national movements. His presence suggested that Jews would make the land of Israel flourish and provide sustenance for its people. At the same time, it expressed a new, contemporary Jew, young and strong, in contrast to the traditional ghetto stereotype or that of the urban Jew who was not at home in nature. The praying figures at the left suggest the traditional roots of the Jewish people in Eretz Israel, and the concept that return to Eretz Israel will afford the traditional Jew the opportunity to pray and learn in the homeland. Surprisingly, a nun is depicted in the foreground

In addition to designing the Second Congress postcard and delegate card, Okin produced Zionist drawings which were published in *Die Welt*.

CAT. NO. 36

*37. Reden gehalten auf dem
II Zionisten Congress zu Basel
(Speeches from the II Zionist Congress at
Basel)*

Vienna: Buchdruckerei "Industrie" 1898
9 x 5 5/8 in

Zionist leaders realized it was important to disseminate information regarding the proceedings
at the Congresses. This pamphlet contains copies
of speeches delivered at the Second Congress by
Herzl, Nordau, Mandelstamm and Rabbi Gaster.
The cover decoration includes the Magen David
(Star of David) framing a map of Eretz Israel.

*38. Comfort of Zion From the Second Zionist
Congress in Basel and the Speeches of Max
Nordau (Yiddish and Russian)*

Warsaw: S. Bromberg, 1898
7 1/4 x 5 1/4 in.

*39. Postcard: A Happy New Year
(Hebrew and English)
2ND ZIONIST CONGRESS AT BASLE IN 1898*

Hebrew Publishing Co. No. 50
New York
Postmark Sep. 22 1911
3 1/2 x 5 1/2 in.

This image is based on a painting by Menahem
Okin showing Theodor Herzl and Max Nordau
shaking hands at the opening of the Second Zionist Congress; Herzl wanted speakers and delegates
to wear formal dress to the Congress sessions. The
rationale was twofold: by wearing the same attire,
their social status would not be visible and the
importance of the occasion would be emphasized.
This attire would also suggest to the viewer that
Jewish leaders are financially well-to-do, powerful, serious, established, and therefore worthy of
the respect and attention of world leaders.

*40. Geschäftsordnung der Zionisten-Congresse
(Proceedings of the Zionist Congress)*

Verlag des Zionisten-Congresses in Basel
Vienna: Buchdruckerei "Industrie", 1899
8 3/4 x 5 5/8 in.; binding 9 x 5 7/8 in.

*41. The Messenger of Zion
"The Third Basel Congress"*

London, August 1899
9 3/4 x 7 1/4 in.

Contemporary Jewish press reports enthusiasti-
cally covered ceremonies and speeches at the
Zionist Congresses.

*42. Postcard: IV Zionisten Congress August
13–16 1900 5660 London (IV Zionist Congress
August 13–16 1900 5660 London)*

3 1/2 x 5 1/2 in.

An angel with a Magen David (Star of David) halo
shows a group of Jewish exiles in East European
dress the path to an idealized Eretz Israel.

*43. Postcard: V. Zionisten-Congress in Basel
26–30 December 1901 (Fifth Zionist Congress
in Basel; Hebrew and German)*

Hebrew inscription: "Let our eyes witness Your
loving return to Zion" from the Amidah liturgy
Artist: E.M. Lilien (1874–1925)
Postmark Netanya 3.5.73
3 1/2 x 5 1/2 in.

In this drawing, Lilien contrasts the plight of
Eastern European Jews with the freedom and
opportunities of Eretz Israel. A winged angel,
hand on the shoulder of an aged East European
Jew surrounded by barbed wire, points to a vigorous young man ploughing a field of wheat against
a rising sun. Such imagery suggested that Jews
had already accomplished much in Eretz Israel. It
also signified the willingness and ability of Jews to
perform manual labor, in contrast to traditional
anti-semitic stereotypes of the Jew as unsuited to
such tasks.

44. *Two Letters*

Theodor Herzl

Typed and signed by: Ozer Kokesch
(1860–1905), Schriftführer (secretary)
Vienna, December 19, 1903
11 1/2 x 8 3/4 in.
Vienna, 18 June 1903
10 1/2 x 8 1/2 in.

Kokesch was one of the founders of the first
Jewish students' association, Kadimah, at the
Vienna University in 1882. He served as assistant
to Theodor Herzl, and on the committee which
prepared for the First Zionist Congress.

One of these two letters contains a program for
the Sixth Congress. The other letter deals with
Russian Jewish concerns.

45. *Postcard: THEODOR HERZL MIT*
VERTRETERN BEROJUDE
(Theodor Herzl with Representatives from the
Mountains; Hebrew and German)

Early 20th century
3 1/2 x 5 1/2 in.

Representatives of far-flung communities attended the Congresses, and many of them had their
photograph taken in company with Herzl, symbol
of Zionist prestige and power. The local garb worn
by the delegates from the Russian Caucasus contrasts sharply with Herzl's formal European dress.

46. *Postcard: Zionisten-Congress, Basel*
Journalisten (Zionist Congress, Basel
Journalists)

Early 20th century
3 1/2 x 5 1/2 in.

This image shows Herzl at the Sixth Congress,
dressed as usual in dark clothes, in the company
of a group of men and women, some of whom are
less formally attired. While correct attire was
mandatory for those who wished to be socially
acceptable, those who were not concerned with
acceptance or were of a more bohemian inclina-
tion apparently felt free not to conform.

Zionisten-Congress, Basel   Journalisten

CAT. NO. 46

47. *Postcard: Theodor Herzl*
XI Zionisten-Kongress

S. Roukhomovsky
Vienna, 1913
3 1/2 x 5 1/2 in.

A pensive Herzl rests his head on his hand in the
foreground of this image created after his demise;
a copy of *Der Judenstaat* lies on the table near
his elbow. Beyond, a female personification of
Zionism unchained, modeled after the female per-
sonifications of German and French nationalist
movements, points the way to Eretz Israel to
Eastern European Jewish refugees. The use of
Herzl's image suggests the continued authority of
his program for the Zionist future in Eretz Israel
as outlined in *Der Judenstaat*.

48. *Shekel Certificate*

No. 1216
Ha Poel Ha-Zair and Zeirei Zion
Romania, 1921
Paper
4 1/4 x 5 1/4 in.

A selection of shekel certificates from the Anson
collection are on exhibit. These were issued as
membership cards in the Zionist organization after
payment of a fee. Until 1960, the number of
shekels sold in a country was used to calculate the
number of the country's delegates to the Congress. The idea was born at the First Zionist
Congress (1897); the shekel was a standard coin
in Eretz Israel during the Biblical period, and its
collection was referred to in the Bible as a way of
counting the Jewish people.

49. Postcard: JOSEPH BEI DEN ISMAELITERN (Joseph among the Ishmaelites)

Artist: Lesser Ury (1861–1931)
[Official Postcard of the] 12th Zionist Congress
Carlsbad, 1921
3 1/2 x 5 1/2 in.

Lesser Ury was one of the artists whose works were exhibited in conjunction with the Fifth Congress, at which Martin Buber delivered a lecture on the importance of Jewish art in the Zionist movement.

Ury was a melancholy recluse who resided in Berlin. At the time that he produced this design, his work, especially his scenes of Berlin, was on its way to becoming popular and commanding high prices.

50. Postcard: ALTER JUDE MIT THORAROLLE (Old Jew with Torah Scroll)

Artist: Jacob Steinhardt (1887–1968)
[Official Postcard of the] 12th Zionist Congress
Carlsbad, 1921
Postmark Karlovy, 7.IX.21
5 1/2 x 3 1/2 in.

This illustration maintains the tradition in Zionist art which contrasted elderly religious figures with strong young pioneers. The continued practice of producing artworks as Congress postcards shows that Zionist leaders still felt it necessary to demonstrate that Jews were not only capable of producing art, but were actively doing so.

Steinhardt studied engraving under Hermann Struck (1876–1944). His work is related to that of contemporary German expressionists. At this time, he still resided in Berlin. Later, he moved to Jerusalem and became head of Bezalel's graphic department.

51. Postcard: View of Prague

[Official postcard of the]
18th Zionist Congress
Postmark 17 August 1933
3 1/2 x 5 1/2 in.

Views of the city in which a Congress was held were popular subjects for official postcards. Cards were customized by the addition of the number and dates of the Congress, so that even those which were not mailed retained their Congress connection.

52. Congress pass #2067

18th Zionist Congress
Issued by Hans Meiss Travelbureau Zurich,
Prague, 1933
5 x 3 in.

The Eighteenth Zionist Congress, held in Prague, was marked by the rise of Nazism in Germany and the beginning of the anti-Jewish campaign.

53. Stick Pin

18th Zionist Congress
Prague, 1933
Copper, enamel
2 1/4 x 3/4 in.

Pins continued to identify delegates to the Congresses. This example is decorated with the Hebrew number eighteen and a Magen David against a bright blue background.

54. Postcard: Zionist Congress

Postmark Vienna, 7.IX.1935
5 3/4 x 4 1/4 in.

This meeting of the National Zionist Organization was held in Vienna three days after the September 4th closing of the Nineteenth Zionist Congress in Lucerne. Drawing on the visual vocabulary of Social Realism, the artist depicts a stark chained hand holding aloft a menorah to call attention to the contemporary plight of the Jewish people.

55. Pin

22nd Zionist Congress
Basel, 1946
Paper disc on metal pin
D: 1 in.

This was the first Congress convened after the Holocaust, held December 9-24, 1946 in Basel.

56. Postcard: The Convention Hall under Construction

23rd Zionist Congress
Jerusalem, 1951
4 x 5 3/4 in.

The 23rd Zionist Congress, the second after the Holocaust, was held in the new State of Israel. The construction of a hall to house subsequent Congresses was a powerful symbol of the success of the Zionist cause. To further mark the occasion, the opening ceremony was held at the new Herzl gravesite, underlining Herzl's continued importance in the construction of Zionist identity.

57. First Day Cover envelope and stamp 23rd Zionist Congress

Postmark Jerusalem 14.8.1951
3 3/4 x 6 in.

58. Pin resembling Shekel

23rd Zionist Congress
Jerusalem, 1951
D: 1 1/8 in.

The Zionist shekel, based on the Biblical Jewish coin, was a receipt issued on payment of the membership fee. With the establishment of the State, it once again is a unit of Jewish currency.

59. El Al Menu
26th Zionist Congress

Jerusalem, December 30, 1965 – January 13, 1966
6 3/4 x 9 3/4 in.

Delegates to the early Congresses often expressed the feeling that an important part of the experience was the train ride to the Congress, during which one met fellow delegates and began to establish friendships. More recently, this bonding experience begins on the El Al flight to Israel, and special souvenir menus mark the occasion.

60. Souvenir Envelope
The 30th Zionist Congress

Postmark Jerusalem 7.12.82
4 1/2 x 9 in.

Funding and Fundraising

The Jewish Colonial Trust, established in 1899, began operations in 1902 with a capital of 2,000,000 pounds, in shares of one pound each. The Trust handled financial transactions relating to immigration and to development within Eretz Israel. In 1902 the Trust incorporated the Anglo-Palestine Company, now Bank Leumi le-Israel, providing the basis for a modern banking system capable of serving the expanding population. Later, this became the Anglo-Palestine Bank, the central financial institution of the *yishuv* (settlement). Other financial institutions included the Mizrachi Bank.

The issue of financing the Zionist Organization was recognized early. At the First Zionist Congress in 1897, Professor Shapira (1840–1898) proposed a fund to buy land. The Jüdische National Fond (Jewish National Fund; Keren Kayemeth le-Israel) was founded by the 5th Congress in 1901 to purchase and develop land in Eretz Israel. To raise funds it issued stamps and distributed collection boxes (called *pushkes* in Yiddish). Many of these were decorated with the lion and star symbol of the First Zionist Congress. To demonstrate their support for the Zionist cause, people sent Jewish National Fund telegrams and put the stamps on their correspondence, and children collected JNF stamps as they collect stickers today, or received them for good work in school.

Like relics, Herzl's personal possessions were enshrined, visually linking JNF's origins and the Zionist hero, enhancing the organizations claims to authority. Herzl's office, first located in the JNF office in Vienna, and later moved to Israel, appeared on many issues of Zionist postcards.

CAT. NO. 61

61. *Jewish Colonial Trust Certificate #29260*

Issued December 1900
Issued to Nathan Ellenbogen of Troy, New York
Signed by Wolffsohn and Loewy
8 3/4 x 14 3/4 in.

The Zionist movement encompassed both observant as well as non-observant Jews. Zionist imagery reflects these constituencies, depicting Eretz Israel as the site where the "Traditional Jew" and the "Young Zionist" could live in harmony. This certificate is decorated with the Magen David (Star of David) and characteristic images of Jews praying at the Western Wall juxtaposed with Zionist laborers. The certificate represents one share in the Jewish Colonial Trust, one pound of a total capital of 2,000,000 pounds.

62. *Statuten des Jewish Colonial Trust Share Clubs und der Londoner Centrale (Statutes of the Jewish Colonial Trust Share Clubs and the London Centrale)*

Aug. Siegle
London, June 1900
7 1/4 x 5 in.

Although it was established in 1899, the Jewish Colonial Trust did not begin operations until 1902. It handled financial transactions relating to immigration and to development within Eretz Israel.

63. *Debenture No. 264*

Frcs. 1000
The Anglo-Palestine Co. Limited
Eretz Israel, 1909–1926
10 1/2 x 12 1/2 in.

This is one of a series of 300 bearer debentures of 1000 Francs each, issued by the Anglo-Palestine Co. Limited. However, it was never used and all the spaces for information regarding purchaser are blank.

64. *Jewish Colonial Trust Stamp Souvenir*

Designed before 1904
2 x 2 1/8 in.

This piece is illustrated in the *Herzl Memorial Album* (1929), where the caption notes that Herzl approved the design before his demise. The upper half of this stamp bears a left profile depiction of Herzl; the lower half has a central Magen David (Star of David).

65. *Check No. 43731 for 200 frs.*

The Anglo-Palestine Company Limited
Jaffa, March 13, 1906
3 3/4 x 8 in.

The Anglo-Palestine Company provided the financial services for the expanding population of the *yishuv* (settlement).

66. *Three Keren Kayemet Herzl Stamps*

Hebrew inscription: If I forget thee, O Jerusalem, let my right hand forget her cunning. (Psalms 137.5)
Cologne, Germany 1909, 2 x 1 1/4 in.
Canada, 1919, 1 1/2 x 1 1/4 in.
1938, 1 1/2 x 1 1/4 in.

This image of Herzl leaning over the balcony of the Three Kings Hotel, adopted from the Lilien photograph, was the second most popular stamp ever issued by JNF.

67. *Postcard: Herzl's Arbeitszimmer im Zion. Kongressburo, Wien, Türkenstrasse 9 (Herzl's Office in the Zionist Congress Office, Vienna, Türkenstrasse 9)*

Herzlichen Glückwunsch zum neuen Jahre!
(Best Wishes for the New Year)
Jüdisher Nationalfonds (Jewish National Fund)
[German and Hebrew]
Künstlerkarte 318 Ser Z.11
Eretz Israel, 1912
3 1/2 x 5 1/2 in.

One element of the social construction of Herzl as Jewish hero was a pilgrimage to his grave (cat. no. 17) and to his office, both originally in Vienna. Postcards depicting these sites functioned as souvenirs of actual visits. For those who could not visit in person but were able to obtain a copy of the image in postcard form, such postcards provided an alternative manner of access to Herzl's symbolic presence, and functioned in place of a real visit.

68. *"Telegram" With Wedding Salutations*

Telegramm abgelöst zu Funsten den Jüdischen Nationalfonds (Telegram for the benefit of the Jewish National Fund)
Karlsruhe, Baden, 18 March 1913
Paper; printed, handwritten
8 1/2 x 9 1/2 in.

Popular fundraising items like this were sold to benefit the Jewish National Fund. Eight of the JNF "Herzl stamps" are glued to this page. The image of Herzl leaning over a balcony was based on a photograph taken by E.M. Lilien in 1901. To this image was added a view of Jerusalem towards the walls of the Old City and the Tower of David. A multitude of figures representing pioneers fill the space between Herzl and the walls. This motif of Herzl leaning over the balcony facing Jerusalem was adopted for domestic objects such as rugs as well as stamps and postcards.

69. One Share in The Mizrahi Bank Ltd. #1448

Issued to Mr. H. Blank
Printed by R. Goldberg
Jerusalem, 1925
10 3/4 x 13 1/8 in.

This certificate represents one share in the Mizrahi Bank, valued at one English pound, of a total capital of 50,000 pounds. The border decoration, perhaps influenced by the work of the Bezalel School, shows the influence of Islamic arabesque and the sinuous flowing lines of European Art Nouveau.

One of the signatures on this certificate is that of Hermann Struck (1876–1944), the graphic artist known for his illustrations of Jewish life. He joined the Zionist movement in 1903, and met Theodor Herzl, a meeting which inspired the Zionist leader's portrait (cat. nos. 199 and 201).

70. Fundraising Stamp Booklet

JNF QUIZ REPLIES 99 STAMPS
ISSUED BY HEBREW EDUCATORS' COUNCIL
FOR JEWISH NATIONAL FUND
[Hebrew and English]
New York, ca. 1949
Cost of series $1.65
5 3/4 x 3 7/8 in.

In a children's fundraising contest held by the Hebrew Educators' Council, contestants had to acquire all 99 stamps from this booklet. The series could be purchased for $1.65; a row of three stamps cost 5¢. The proceeds collected were applied to the Palestine Land Redemption work of the Jewish National Fund.

71. Oval Sticker

Hebrew inscription: Binyamin Zeev Herzl 1860–1904; 50 years since his death
Keren Kayemet Le-Israel
2 x 1 1/8 in.

The most common JNF promotional material consisted of stamps distributed in return for contributions, for which Herzl's image was a popular motif.

72. Folding New Year's Greeting

Keren Kayemet Le-Israel
Hebrew inscription: A good and blessed year; A year of settlement and Aliyah, peace and produce
1955
3 3/4 x 6 3/4 in.

Much Zionist fundraising imagery continued to focus on agriculture and its role in the development of the State of Israel.

73. Postcard: HERZL ROOM [Hebrew and English]

The Herzl Room Rebuilt at JNF Headquarters in Jerusalem
Israel, postmark 25.4.56
4 x 6 in.

The transfer of the interior of Herzl's office from Vienna to the headquarters of the Jewish National Fund in Jerusalem visually confirmed the Zionist achievement, and symbolized the continuation of Herzl's work by the JNF in Jerusalem.

74. Jewish National Fund Stamps Commemorating the Centennial of Herzl's Birth

"Happy New Year" [Hebrew]
1960
Postcard
4 1/2 x 6 3/4 in.

The decades and centennials of Herzl's birth and death were marked by special fundraising efforts, particularly on the part of Zionist organizations such as JNF.

The Dawn of Statehood

In 1948 when David Ben Gurion proclaimed the State of Israel, he stood under a portrait of Herzl, emphasizing the fact that the creation of the State was the culmination of Herzl's vision and the Zionist effort. This was followed in 1949 by the transfer of Herzl's body from Vienna to Israel, and its ceremonial re-interment. The pageantry surrounding the reburial following the creation of the State of Israel further underscored Herzl's position as a Jewish hero, while serving as a metaphor which would remind people that the establishment of this State was the culmination of the Zionist dream he articulated. This gave Herzl's monument a new dimension of significance and power and paid tribute to Herzl as founding father of the State. The military cemetery on the north slope reinforces its image as a resting place for those who gave their lives to make Israel a reality.

This site, on a mountain renamed Mount Herzl, became the focus of pilgrimage by Zionists, just as the old site in Vienna had been. It represents a point of access to the hero and to his achievement. In the same fashion, the transfer of Herzl's office to the JNF office symbolically reminded people that Zionism received its authority from Herzl, as if he had been a prophet and his possessions held an aura of sanctity. Today, visits to both these sites take on an almost ritual character, acknowledging the sacrifice made by this almost mythic being for the Zionist cause, and functioning as both a celebration of the connection between past and present, and of the history of the Jewish people and their recent triumph. Images of the reburial, the tomb in Israel, and the new installation of Herzl's office were added to the iconography of Zionism.

75. *Ha'Aretz*
"The Decision to Establish the Jewish State"
Vol. 30
November 30, 1947
Newspaper
22 1/2 x 17 in.

The prominence of Herzl's image in the press at the time of the establishment of the State of Israel celebrates the Zionist achievement and the continuity between the Zionist past and present.

76. *"The People Prepare for the Government of Israel"*
Independence Day Edition
Joint edition of Israeli newspapers
Friday 5 Iyar 5708 4 pm. (May 14, 1948)
Newspaper
22 1/2 x 17 in.; framed 25 3/4 x 19 3/4 in.

The production of a joint edition of Israeli newspapers for this momentous event was in itself a symbol of its importance. The use of Herzl's image demonstrates how tightly his image was woven into the political fabric of the State of Israel, while confirming the achievement of the goal for which he gave his life.

77. *Plaque*
Declaration of Independence of the State of Israel
Copyright Grodel Inc.
New York, 1948
Brass
13 1/4 x 10 1/2 in.

Herzl's image prominently gazes at the viewer from the top center of this plaque, a juxtaposition which symbolically binds the new State of Israel to the Zionist past.

78. Souvenir Program for the Jews of Vienna on the occasion of Herzl's coffin leaving for Israel

Published by H. Halpern
Vienna, Sunday August 14, 1949
8 1/4 x 6 in.

This program includes an image of the decorative cover which draped Herzl's coffin during the transfer, and subsequently disappeared. Although Herzl's coffin was taken to Israel, the grave marker in Vienna was preserved, and continues to be venerated.

CAT. NO. 79

79. Pin
Hebrew inscriptions: Honor guard carrying Herzl's coffin, 1949; "...and you shall carry my bones from here with you"
(Exodus 13.19)

Silver
Israel, 1949
D: 1 in.

The Hebrew letters forming the texts constitutes the primary decoration of this simple badge, worn by one of the honor guards assigned to carry rather than merely escort Herzl's casket. The quotation from Exodus provides a historical precedent for the request made by Herzl to transfer his remains. The Biblical patriarch Jacob died in the land of Egypt and before his death he extracted from his sons the promise that they would carry his bones to the Land of Israel when they returned.

80. Two Photographs of Herzl's Re-interment

Inscriptions reverse: Lars (?) Berger 3 XI 1949
HERZL BURIAL
Jerusalem, 1949
Black and white
2 1/2 x 3 1/4 in.

Many private individuals attended the ceremonial re-interment of Herzl in Israel. These photographs are rare personal souvenirs of that occasion.

81. Two Souvenirs of Attendance at Re-interment of Herzl
Keren Kayemet le-Israel

Collection of Morton Axelrod
4 x 1 in. ea.

82. Musical Card—Declaration of Independence at the Tel-Aviv Museum Record—The National Hymn—Hatikvah

Produced by Polyphon
Israel, ca. 1950s–60s
Color Postcard
6 1/2 x 8 in.

Dual-function postcards, which could be played like a record and conveyed both a visual and an auditory message, were popular during this period when record players were ubiquitous.

CAT. NO. 82

Stamps

During the British Mandate, pictorial stamps were issued representing historical sites in Eretz Israel, inscribed with the name "Palestine" in English, Hebrew and Arabic. Used from 1927 through 1948, these images include: Rachel's Tomb, the Dome of the Rock and the Tower of David. During the War of Independence, supplies of postage stamps often ran out and stamps had to be improvised. Often Jewish National Fund labels were used, overprinted with the word *Doar* (Post). The State of Israel began issuing stamps on June 20, 1948. Several of these stamps and cancellations incorporate the features of Theodor Herzl, a visual statement emphasizing the connection between Zionism and Israel. Recent productions reproduce popular Zionist imagery, including the Lilien image of Herzl on the balcony and a shekel certificate, and Zionist material culture artifacts such as the rug with Herzl's portrait.

83. Envelope with Keren Kayemet Stamps

Hebrew inscription: National Leadership
Postmark Kefar Ata
5 x 6 in.

Two JNF Herzl stamps were used on this envelope mailed to Tel-Aviv during the War of Independence, a common occurrence when supplies of stamps ran out.

84. Envelope with Image of Herzl

First Day of Opening Tel-Aviv
Post Office in Israel
Postmark Tel Aviv 16.5.1948
5 x 6 in.

This is the earliest envelope in the Anson collection with an image of Herzl. It bears a small left profile of Herzl in an oval frame, accompanied by texts of the Balfour and 1947 Declarations, a visual encoding of the concept that Herzl's work fathered the Balfour Declaration and the foundation of the State of Israel.

CAT. NO. 85

85. Envelope with Image of Herzl

Hebrew inscriptions: If you will it it is no dream: 14.2.1896 Herzl; First anniversary of United Nations decision
Postmark Tel Aviv 29.11.1948
5 x 6 in.

A strong image of Herzl's left profile adorns this commemorative envelope. The map on one of the two stamps shows the partition recommended by the United Nations Special Committee on Palestine (UNSCOP), which isolated Jerusalem as an International Zone. The dark regions on this map mark the territory the committee suggested be allotted to the Jews.

86. Envelope depicting Keren Kayemet

Herzl Stamp
Postmark Tel Aviv 4.5.49
5 x 6 in.

The Herzl stamp, a popular Zionist material culture artifact, decorates this early State of Israel postal envelope, a visual statement linking the State to the Zionist movement.

87. First Day Cover with image of Herzl after Struck engraving

Postmark Haifa 31.3.1949
4 x 7 in.

A famous image of Herzl by Hermann Struck (1876–1944) was used to decorate this early Israeli commemorative envelope.

88. Envelope with Image of Herzl

Hebrew: Binyamin Zeev Herzl Day of reinterment
Postmark Tel Aviv 17.8.1949
4 1/2 x 5 3/4 in.

The image on this envelope reproduces the popular Lilien image of Herzl on the balcony at the Three Kings Hotel.

89. Envelope with Image of Herzl

Hebrew and English: 47th Anniversary of Herzl's Death
Postmark Tel Aviv-Jaffa 24.7.1951
3 5/8 x 6 in.

The first Zionist Congress to be held in Israel opened in August 1951; this envelope depicts the JNF Herzl stamp which incorporated Lilien's motif of Herzl on the balcony of the Three Kings Hotel at the time of the Fifth Zionist Congress.

90. First Day Cover

Hebrew: Dr. Binyamin Zeev Herzl
Fiftieth Anniversary of His Death
Stamp and envelope designed by E. Errell
Lithographed, printed by Lewin-Epstein
Issued July 21, 1954, withdrawn June 20, 1955
Postmark Jerusalem 21.7.54
4 x 6 in.

The ceremonial lying-in-state of the coffin of Theodor Herzl at the time of his reinterment is reproduced on this envelope. The stamp, which depicts Herzl, was designed by E. Errell in honor of the 50th anniversary of Herzl's death.

91. JEWISH NATIONAL FUND ISSUE 1904–1954
SOUVENIR OF THE SOCIETY OF ISRAEL PHILATELISTS
SIXTH ANNUAL ISRAEL STAMP EXHIBIT
November 19-20-21 1954

ASDA Show
71 St. Regiment Armory
New York, November 19–20–21 1954
Postcard
3 1/2 x 5 3/4 in.

This philatelic souvenir incorporates a stamp depicting an idyllic view of Israel juxtaposed against an image of the JNF Herzl stamp, and a printed left profile image of Herzl. Issued by JNF, the card portrays Herzl as hero who made possible the State of Israel, and all its current glories.

92. Envelope
Hebrew and English: S.S. Theodor Herzl
Maiden Voyage
With Compliments from Zim

Zim Israel Navigation Co.
Postmark Jerusalem 23.5.57
4 x 6 in.

The Israel Navigation Company, Zim, was established in 1945 to run both passenger and cargo ships. This envelope bears a depiction of the S.S. Theodor Herzl flying two flags, one the former

Zionist banner now the flag of the State of Israel, the other bearing seven stars alluding to the seven hour work day suggested by Herzl.

CAT. NO. 93

93. Envelope
S.S. THEODOR HERZL
MAIDEN VOYAGE FROM HAIFA
POST OPENING ON BOARD S.S. THEODOR
HERZL 23rd MAY 1957

Postmark S.S. Theodor Herzl 23.5.57
5 x 6 in.

During the first twenty years of the State, most people travelled to Israel by ship. In common with lavish hotels and other ocean liners of the period, the S. S. Theodor Herzl made available souvenir envelopes and postcards depicting the ship itself; mail was postmarked on the ship.

94. Envelope with Three Israeli Stamps depicting Herzl

Envelope inscribed: LA MAISON OÙ NAQUIT HERZL, ET LA SYNAGOGUE, À BUDAPEST (The house where Herzl was born, and the Synagogue, at Budapest)
Postmark Jerusalem 31.8.60
4 x 6 in.

23rd Zionist Congress Stamp
Designed by Maxime and Gabriel Shamir
Printed by Lewin-Epstein
Issued August 14, 1951,
Withdrawn March 15, 1953

Stamp in honor of the 50th Anniversary of Herzl's Death
Designed by E. Errell
Lithographed, printed by Lewin-Epstein
Issued July 21, 1954,
Withdrawn June 20, 1955

Stamp commemorating the centennial of Herzl's birth
Designed by Maxime and Gabriel Shamir
Lithographed, printed by Lewin-Epstein
Issued August 31, 1960,
Withdrawn February 3, 1962
Stamped Day of Issue, 1960

Two of these stamps bear realistic images of Herzl. The one designed by the Shamir brothers in 1960 is based on Lilien's image of Herzl on the balcony; Errell's image pairs Herzl with seven stars for the seven hour work day he suggested. The 1951 Shamir design is less realistic and more sculptural than the other two. The Shamirs designed medals and Israeli banknotes as well as postage stamps.

95. Postcard: First Day Cover

Publisher: Simon's Maximum Card
Postmark Tel Aviv 31.8.60
6 x 3 3/4 in.

This colored reinterpretation of Lilien's image of Herzl leaning over the balcony of the Three Kings Hotel was produced in 1960 for the Herzl stamp designed by M. & G. Shamir, which also depicts Herzl on the balcony.

96. First Day Cover

Hebrew and English: BENJAMIN ZEEV HERZL
Stamp: Israel 30 Years of Independence; Dr. TH.
Herzl 1860–1904
Postmark Jerusalem 4.7.78
4 x 6 3/4 in.

This envelope, designed as a first day cover, reproduces the full-face image of Herzl depicted on the stamp.

97. Postcards with Series of Herzl Stand By Stamps

Postmark Jerusalem, 1.1.86
4 x 6 in. each

This series of stamps depicts Herzl's left profile. This series represents denominations of 1, 2, 3, 5, 10 and 20 Agorot; the color of the postcard matches the color of the number on each stamp.

98. First Day Cover

Theodor Herzl
Jerusalem, January 1986
5 x 7 1/2 in.

This envelope reproduces the left profile view of Herzl from the stamp. It bears the full eight stamps issued, in denominations of 1, 2, 3, 5, 10, 20, 30 and 50 Agorot.

99. Souvenir Leaf

Jewish National Fund 90th Anniversary
1901–1991
Israel Postal Authority, Philatelic Service
No. 2996
1991
8 x 5 1/2 in.

The popular JNF Herzl stamp is reproduced on this souvenir leaf, a continued reminder of the organization's importance in Zionist history.

100. Envelope with Shekel Stamp #1338 and 1954 JNF stamp of Stadt-Casino, Basel

Postmark Basel 19.12.91
4 1/4 x 7 in.

The shekel stamp, which depicts the First Congress shekel, an artifact of Zionist popular culture, was issued in two pieces; the bottom half depicts Herzl.

101. First Day Cover

Theodor Herzl Der Judenstaat
Israel Postal Authority
Postmark Jerusalem 3.9.1996
3 7/8 x 6 3/4 in.

An early two color JNF stamp depicts the Basel Casino, a familiar Zionist landmark, site of the First Zionist Congress. This first day cover bears an elaborate contemporary multicolored image of the Casino in five sections; the stamp itself is the central section.

102. Theodor Herzl Der Judenstaat

Stamp depicting wall hanging with Herzl's image
Israel Postal Authority
Postmark Jerusalem 3.9.1996
3 7/8 x 6 3/4 in.

This stamp depicting an artifact of Zionist popular culture; a wall hanging depicting Herzl, based on Lilien's balcony image. The hanging (cat. no. 150) was created in Eretz Israel at the Alliance Israelite Universelle School.

Coins and Medals

Portraits and exploits of rulers and individuals known for their accomplishments have been commemorated on medals and currency since the Renaissance. Medals serve to familiarize people with the features of relgious and political figures; important current events were also commemorated in this medium. By the early nineteenth century, souvenir medals in a variety of materials including gold, bronze and silver were mass produced easily and inexpensively. Few Jewish medals survive from before the Emancipation period, however, their numbers begin to rise in the late eighteenth century and increase dramatically by the end of the nineteenth century, due to the combined effect of Emancipation and the Industrial Revolution throughout Europe. Commemorative medals were struck portraying notable contemporary Jews, and political and social events important to the members of individual communities, such as the openings of synagogues and charitable organizations. By the late nineteenth century, many Jews were involved in the production of such medals.

The first important Zionist medal was made by Samuel Friedrich Beer for the Second Zionist Congress. Subsequently, many medals were produced with Zionist themes, often incorporating the image of Theodor Herzl. Their number increased with the creation of the State of Israel; several mark anniversaries of its creation. Today there is an official government agency producing commemoratives—The Israel Government Coins and Medals Corporation. The Bank of Israel has also produced a number of Herzl coins, including gold coins struck in 1960 to mark the centenary of Herzl's birth.

The Bezalel School in Jerusalem was a center for Jewish art in Eretz Israel, where art was created for European and American markets. Its founder, Boris Schatz, was personally acquainted with Theodor Herzl, and produced two memorial medals: one of these pairs Herzl with Moses while the other depicts Jews mourning for Herzl. The latter makes an interesting comparison with Schatz's monumental painting on the same subject in the Museum's collection (cat. no. 21).

The Anson collection includes medals depicting figures important in Herzl's life, and those who influenced or were influenced by Herzl. Among these are several medals relating to the Dreyfus Affair, Herzl's first adult encounter with anti-semitism, and a number of coins and medals representing Kaiser Wilhelm II, particularly one commemorating the Kaiser's journey to Jerusalem during which he and Herzl met.

Herzl's portrait was often depicted on medals worn by delegates to conferences. Donors to Zionist organizations were rewarded with pins or medals carrying Herzl's portrait, as were students who excelled in Jewish schools. Among the more popular forms of wearable medals were metal pendants, pins and occasionally even tie clips. Some early examples combine Herzl's features with a Magen David (Star of David), another ubiquitous Zionist symbol. Altogether, over 108 pins and medals (some duplicates of pieces in other metals) from the Anson collection are in the exhibition.

103. Medal
Obverse: *EMILE ZOLA LA VÉRITÉ EST EN MARCHE ET RIEN NE L'ARRETER*
(*Truth has begun and nothing can stop it*)
Reverse: *COLONEL PICQUART JE N'EMPORTERAI PAS CE SERCRET DANS LA TOMBE* (*I will not take this secret to the grave*)

France, late 19/early 20th century
Bronze
1 1/2 x 1 1/4 in.

The French novelist Emile Zola (1840–1902) championed Dreyfus, whom he believed to be innocent. His famous article in Dreyfus' defense, "J'Accuse," was published in *L'Aurore* (January 13, 1898), and resulted in Zola being tried for libel.

Lieutenant-Colonel Marie-Georges Picquart (1854–1914) discovered evidence which would clear Dreyfus, and unsuccessfully attempted to have his superior officers re-open the Dreyfus case.

104. Medal
Obverse: *DREYFUS*
Reverse: *LABORI*

France, late 19th/early 20th century
Bronze
D: 7/8 in.

Fernand Labori (1860–1917) was the criminal lawyer who defended Dreyfus at the Rennes trial.

105. Medal
Obverse: *WILHELM II. KAISER AUGUSTA VICTORIA KAISERIN V. DEUTSCHLAND*
Reverse: *ZUR ERINNERUNG AN DIE KAISERREISE JERUSALEM 1898*

Germany, 1898
Bronze
D: 1 1/4 in.

Kaiser Wilhelm came to Jerusalem to pay a ceremonial visit to the Protestant Church of the Redeemer; during this trip, he met with Herzl.

106. Second Congress Medal
Artist: Samuel Friedrich Beer (1846–1912)

Hebrew inscription: "…I am going to take the Israelite people from among the nations…and bring them to their own land." (Ezekiel 37.21)
1898
Bronze
D: 2 1/2 in.

The earliest and most famous Zionist medal is this one, designed by Beer. The obverse depicts a group of figures in a landscape. A female figure in classical drapery, reminiscent of the figures used to represent Britannia and Germania, places her hand on the shoulder of a man in the group, and points to the rising sun in the distance. The August 15, 1898 edition of *Die Welt* printed an illustration of this medal, and described the scene as Zionism pointing the way to Eretz Israel to Jewish exiles. Although female figures pointing the way to Eretz Israel would recur in some Zionist images, they were never a popular motif. A copy of this medal in silver is also in the Anson collection.

107. Medal Depicting Important Figures of the Second Zionist Congress: Herzl, Gaster, Lazare, Nordau, and Mandelstamm

Yiddish inscription reverse:
Executive council of the Second Zionist Congress in Basel 12 Elul 28–30 August 1898
Hebrew inscription:
"...I am going to take the Israelite people from among the nations...and bring them to their own land." (Ezekiel 37.21)
Bronze, traces of gilt
D: 1 1/4 in.

Portraits of four leaders of the Zionist movement are depicted on this medal, surrounding the face of Theodor Herzl. The reverse shows the Magen David, chosen as a symbol because it lacked religious associations that might make some Jews wary of associating with the movement. The leaders represent both traditional and secular Jews, stressing the unity of the movement and the ability of all Jews to work together for the Zionist cause.

108. Pin in the Shape of a Magen David with central profile of Herzl

Metal, enamel
Late 19th/early 20th century
7/8 x 1/2 in.

This unusual pin combines a Magen David enameled in Zionist blue and white, the colors of the Zionist banner borrowed from those of the tallit, with a central profile portrait of Herzl. Mr. Anson dates this pin to the 1930s.

109. Pin in the Shape of a Magen David

Late 19th/early 20th century
D: 1 in.

Pins and badges such as this Zionist Youth organization lapel pin served to reinforce a sense of community among members of an organization.

110. Memorial Medal

Boris Schatz (1867–1932)
Hebrew inscription Kel Maleh Rahamim...
Theodor Herzl...
Eretz Israel, early 20th century
Copper
Framed 11 1/4 x 9 1/8 in.

Schatz, founder of the Bezalel School, created this powerful image of mourning which incorporates both text and image, a medallic version of his painting (cat. no. 21).

A group of mourners, all male, in various poses, gather around a table on which lies an open book. This is framed at right and left by a lighted candle, evocative of the yahrzeit candle lit on the anniversary of a death In the upper left corner is a Magen David inscribed "Zion," a popular Zionist motif best known from the JNF Zion stamp. This is balanced at the upper right by a profile portrait of Herzl. The composition of this medal is similar to that of Schatz's 1915 medal, Ninth of Av, which also deals with the theme of mourning.

111. Pin

Hebrew Inscription: Herzl
Reverse: MADE IN PALESTINE
Possibly produced at Bezalel
Eretz Israel, early 20th century
Silver
1 3/4 x 1/2 in.

Herzl's left profile is flanked on each side by a Magen David.

112. Stick Pin

Early 20th century
Brass, paper
1 1/2 x 7/16 in.

Inexpensive reproduction techniques enabled pins such as this example with a central image of Herzl to be available to a broad spectrum of the Zionist population.

113. Medal

Moses Murro (1888–1957)
Hebrew inscription: Herzl
Eretz Israel, early 20th century
Bronze
2 x 3 1/4 in.

Murro, who studied at the Bezalel School from 1921, created this image of Herzl symbolically overseeing workers in Eretz Israel.

114. Congress Stick Pin

After medal by Murro
Silver
Early 20th century
1 1/4 x 3/4 in.

Murro's image of Herzl symbolically overseeing the productive work occurring in Eretz Israel (cat. no. 113), was used as a Congress badge.

115. Medal

Artist: Fred J. Kormis 1894–1986
Obverse: DR. THEODOR HERZL
Bronze
2 1/2 x 2 in.

Kormis, a resident of England, is known for producing portrait plaques of famous Jews, among them many Zionist figures. This image of Herzl is not strictly a left profile. By adding stylish twists to Herzl's mustache, Kormis makes him appear more stylish and less like a Biblical prophet. This plaque probably dates from the 1920s, and was illustrated in the memorial album edited by Weisgal.

116. Stick Pin Depicting Herzl's Original Tomb

Hebrew inscription: Grave of Herzl K[eren] K[ayemet] l[e-Israel]
Brass
2 x 3/4 in.

Herzl's grave was a popular site for Zionist pilgrimage. Zionist organizations, particularly JNF, continually incorporated images of Herzl, his tomb and his office, into items they produced, visibly basing their claim to authority on their origin during Herzl's lifetime. A version of this pin was reproduced in Weisgal, so it was probably produced before 1929 when the book was published.

CAT. NO. 115

117. Delegate's Medal with Ribbon

Inscription: If You Will It It is no Legend 49
annual convention
Convention held in Pittsburg, PA 1940
Producer: National Badge & Emblem Co
New York, 1940
Brass: silver plated
4 x 1 3/4 in. with ribbon

Sometimes, as here, medals were combined with colorful ribbons and used as delegate badges.

118. Silver Ingot

Copy of Herzl 60 Agorot Stamp produced for
23rd Zionist Congress in 1951
A.G. Mint #0147
1 Troy Ounce .999 fine silver
2 x 1 in; case 4 3/4 x 3 3/4 in.

The 23rd Zionist Congress Stamp designed by Maxime and Gabriel Shamir was issued August 14, 1951. This ingot reproduces the Shamirs' sculptural left profile view of Herzl.

119. Tie pin in the shape of a Key

Hebrew inscription: Herzl Room
K[eren] K[ayemet] L[e-Israel]
Reverse: HERZL ROOM JERUSALEM
Israel, ca. 1950
Brass
1/2 x 2 1/2 in.

The mundane artifacts which belonged to Herzl's study in Vienna were moved to JNF headquarters in Jerusalem, where they express the derivation of JNF's authority from Herzl. At the same time, they permit visitors to experience a sense of immediacy and access to Herzl and the Zionist movement.

120. Pin

Hebrew inscription: Gathering of Zionist Youth
Jerusalem 1954
Israel, 1954
Tin
1 1/4 x 3/4 in.

The importance of youth in the Zionist movement continues to be emphasized.

121. Medal

Sculptor: Samuel Kretschmer (1894–1972)
Hebrew inscription: Herzl Gymnasium
1900–1959
Israel
Bronze
D: 1 3/4 in.

The Gymnasium School, one of many structures named in memory of Theodor Herzl, was a symbol of the Zionist achievement in Eretz Israel, and the Jewish education it offered. In addition to secular subjects (science) and crafts (woodworking), the school offered Bible in modern Hebrew, demonstrating suppport for the concept that the Hebrew language was a part of the new Jewish national identity.

122. 5 Lirot Coin

Israel, 1960
Silver
D: 1 1/4 in.

The centennial of Herzl's birth was commemorated in this Israeli coin.

123. 20 Israeli Lirot Coin

Sculptors: Miriam Karoli (obverse)
Hebrew inscription obverse: It Is Not A Dream
Reverse: Israel 1860–1960 (Hebrew and English)
Issuer: Bank of Israel
Producer: Government Mint, Berne, Switzerland
Israel 1960
Gold 916 2/3 0/00; 7.988 gm.
D: 3/4 in.

Special commemorative coins have been issued in Israel on numerous occasions. One was the anniversary of Herzl's birth, marked by the issue of this 20 lirot gold coin, the first gold coin minted in Israel. By issuing this coin, Israel also celebrated the achievement of the Zionist dream and the twelfth anniversary of the State of Israel.

124. Pendant

Obverse: 1860–1960 THEODOR HERZL;
Herzl (Hebrew)
Reverse: ISRAEL (Hebrew and English)
14 MAI 1948
Holland, 1960
Gold
1 1/4 x 1 in.

Herzl's left profile on the obverse of this medal is balanced on the reverse by a seven-branched menorah flanked by a Magen David on each side. The menorah, an ancient Jewish symbol, is here juxtaposed with the more recent symbol to celebrate the twelfth anniversary of the creation of the State of Israel and the centennial of Herzl's birth.

125. Herzl Centennial Medal

Obverse: It is no Legend
Hebrew and Spanish inscription reverse:
CENTENARIO DE HERZL (Herzl Centennial)
1860–1960 Keren Kayemet le-Israel Zionist
Federation
Mexico, 1960
Silver
D: 1 3/8 in.

This piece from Mexico is among the many medals created to celebrate the centennial of Herzl's birth. It also reminds the viewer that the Zionist organization and the Jewish National Fund originated at the time of Herzl.

126. Herzl Centennial Medal

Hebrew inscription Obverse:
If You Will It It is no Dream 1860–1960
Yiddish Inscription Reverse: Yiddish School in
Mexico on the Hundredth Birthday of Dr. B.Z.
Herzl; CIMA
Mexico, 1960
Silver plate
D: 1 1/2 in.

Jewish institutions all over the world issued special medals celebrating the Herzl centennial.

127. Medal

Artist: Dodo Shenhav
Obverse: OUR WILL WAS NO LEGEND
(Hebrew and English)
Reverse: LIBERATION OF JERUSALEM 7.6.1967
(Hebrew and English)
Bronze
D: 1 in.

By paraphrasing Herzl, this commemorative links the liberation of Jerusalem to the Zionist past and associates the military achievement of the State of Israel with the Zionist vision.

128. Medal

Artists: Dodo Shenhav; M. Nov
Obverse: OUR WILL WAS NO LEGEND
(Hebrew and English)
Reverse: A NATIONAL HOME FOR THE JEWISH
PEOPLE BALFOUR (Hebrew and English) PAR-
LIAMENT HOUSE 1917–1967
Edge: 4187
Issuer: Shekel Mint
Jerusalem, Israel 1967
Tombac
D: 1 1/4 in.

Until 1966, the Knesset met in a building in Jerusalem originally designed as a bank. The present Knesset building, designed by J. Klarwein and Dov Karmi, opened in 1966. This medal was issued to celebrate that opening and the 50th anniversary of the Balfour Declaration. Copies of this medal in silver and bronze are also in the collection.

129. Medal

Obverse: DAVID BEN GURION PROMULGATOR AND FIRST PRIME MINISTER OF THE NEW ISRAEL
Reverse: HOW BEAUTIFUL ARE THY TENTS O JACOB, THY DWELLINGS, O ISRAEL! NUM.24.52 (Hebrew and English); Wenn ihr wollt ist es kein Marchen TH. HERZL 1948 (If you will it is no dream)
Holland, 1968
Silver
D: 1 1/4 in.

Past and present, Zionism and the State of Israel, are all honored in this medal which is inscribed with a Biblical quotation as well as Herzl's famous words.

130. Medal

Artist: Samuel Kretschmer (1894–1972)
Obverse: IT IS NO LEGEND HERZL (Hebrew and English)
Reverse: ISRAEL'S 20TH ANNIVERSARY 1948–1968 (Hebrew and English)
Israel, 1968
Bronze; silver plate
D: 2 1/4 in.

This medal celebrating the twentieth anniversary of the State of Israel incorporates Herzl's famous quotation. It shows that Herzl continued to be bound to the concept and achievements of the State of Israel in the minds of those who produced and commissioned the medal, and illustrates the continued importance of Zionism in the State of Israel and the centrality of Herzl's image in the expression of Zionist identity. We see the familiar left profile, crowned by seven stars, reminding us that Herzl was the visionary who provided the driving spirit behind the foundation of the State, as well as an early advocate of a seven hour work day.

131. Medal

I. ZANGWILL
ENGLISH AUTHOR WHO IMMORTALIZED WITH HUMOR THE STORY OF JEWISH GHETTO LIFE IN 18TH CENTURY LONDON AIDED RISE OF BRITISH ZIONISM 1868–1926
Franklin Mint, 1969–1975
Bronze
D: 1 3/4

Between 1969 and 1975, the Franklin Mint produced a series of medals, known as the Medallic History of the Jewish People, for the Judaic Heritage Society. This set included pioneers and early Zionist leaders up to the time of the resignation of Golda Meir as Prime Minister of Israel. The series was the idea of Robert Weber, who established the offices of the Israel Government Coins and Medals Corporation in North America during the 1960s. (see cat. nos. 131–135)

132. Medal

DREYFUS
VICTIM AND HERO OF THE DREYFUS AFFAIR ALFRED DREYFUS JEW FRENCH ARMY CAPTAIN FALSELY CONVICTED AND IMPRISONED FOR TREASON THEN ABSOLVED. 1859–1935
Franklin Mint, 1969–1975
Silver
D: 1 1/2 in.

133. Medal

LEON PINSKER
PIONEER ZIONIST RUSSIAN JOURNALIST WHO URGED IN HIS AUTOEMANCIPATION NATIONAL REBIRTH OF JEWS ON THEIR OWN INDEPENDENT TERRITORY 1821–1891
Franklin Mint. 1969–1975
D: 1 1/2 in.

134. Medal

Designer: Oscar Harris
Sculptor Caesar Rufo
Reverse: HERZL
VISIONARY FOUNDER OF MODERN POLITICAL
ZIONISM. PROPHET OF A FLOURISHING
JEWISH NATION. "IF YOU WILL IT—IT IS NO
LEGEND". HUNGARIAN-BORN. 1860–1904

Franklin Mint, 1969–1975
Sterling
D: 1 1/2 in.

135. Medal

Obverse: …it is no dream.
Reverse: The Birth Of Israel
Franklin Mint
1969–1975
Sterling Silver
D: 1 1/2 in.

136. 100 Lirot Bank Note #5362194777

Designed by Paul Kor
Bank Israel
Israel, 1973
3 x 5 3/4 in.

This Israeli banknote from 1973 presents a visual
statement of the conception of Herzl as Israeli
hero. It weaves him into the fabric of the State of
Israel, confirming him as the catalyst without
whose efforts it would not exist. At the same time,
the depiction of one of the gates of Jerusalem on
the reverse of the note reminds one of the long
history of Jews in Eretz Israel.

137. Medal

Obverse: IT IS NO LEGEND HERZL
(Hebrew & English)
Reverse: A TIME TO LOVE AND A TIME TO
HATE, A TIME FOR WAR AND A TIME FOR
PEACE ISRAEL 1948 1973 Ecclesiastes 3.1–8
Israel, 1973
Tombac
D: 2 1/2 in.

138. Two Medals

Artist: Elizabeth Jones
Obverse: WANDERERS NO MORE HERZL,
WEIZMANN, MEIR, BEN-GURION
Reverse: ISRAEL A DREAM FULFILLED ISRAEL
(Hebrew)
Producer: Medallic Art Co., #209
Issued by: International Numismatic Agency
New York, 1973
Bronze and silver plated bronze
D: 2 5/8 in. ea.

Jones' medal links contemporary Israeli political
leaders with Herzl.

139. 25th Anniversary of Israel Commemorative Coin

Artist: Clara Weinerth
Hebrew and English inscription (edge):
THE GLORY OF ISRAEL WILL NOT FAIL
English inscription (edge) c[opyright] ART MINT
STERLING PROOF 0527
Israel Government Coins and Medals Corp.
Israel, 1973
Silver
D: 2 in.

A commemoration of the 40th anniversary of the
State of Israel, this piece depicts the declaration
of the State of Israel on May 14, 1948 by David
Ben-Gurion. It clearly depicts the image of Herzl
on the wall beyond Ben-Gurion. The Benno Elkan
menorah, presented to Israel by Great Britain, is
depicted on the reverse of this medal.

The quotation on the edge of this coin comes
from the Bible (I. Samuel 15.29). It brings to mind
thoughts of other heroes of Eretz Israel, known by
the acronym of this verse NILI, *"Nezah Yisrael Lo
Yeshaker"* ("…the Glory of Israel does not
deceive…."). NILI was a spy group under the leadership of Aaron and Sarah Aaronsohn, Avshalom
Feinberg and Yosef Lishansky, operating in Eretz
Israel from 1915 to 1917. The group also aided
Jews expelled from Jaffa and Tel Aviv by the
Turks, and helped transfer financial support to the
yishuv. Aaronsohn was sent by Weizmann to the

U.S., and returned to Eretz Israel in 1918 wih the Zionist Commission.

140. Medal

Hebrew inscription obverse: The Jewish Gymnasium Herzliah 70 years 1906–1976
Hebrew inscription reverse: Teach the youth according to his way (Proverbs 22.6)
Bronze
D: 2 1/4 in.

This medal celebrates the seventieth anniversary of the founding of the Herzl secondary school.

141. Medal

ABRB (Abraham Belskie)
Robert Weber
Obverse: IF YOU WILL IT IT IS NO DREAM
Reverse: SURELY HE SHALL DELIVER THEE (Psalm 91) ENTEBBE RESCUE JULY 4, 1976 YISRAEL (Hebrew)
Medallic Art Co.
Danbury, Connecticut, 1976
Bronze
D: 1 1/2 in.

The use of Herzl's quotation recalls other important achievements of the Jewish people including the rescue of the hijack victims at Entebbe. Taken in conjunction with the quotation from Psalms, it links these accomplishments on a continuum stretching from the historical Jewish past to the triumphant present.

142. Medal Commemorating the First Zionist Congress

Artist: Carter Jones
Reverse: First Zionist Congress
Edge: JUDAIC HERITAGE SOCIETY R[OBERT] W[EBER]
Produced by Medallic Art Co., ca. 1980
Silver plate
1 1/2 x 1 1/2 in

This medal is an unusual, hexagonal shape. On one face, a large portrait of Herzl occupies the foreground, while the famous handshake between Herzl and Nordau which opened the First Congress is depicted in the background. This image is also portrayed on a New Year's greeting card in the exhibition (cat. no. 39). The reverse depicts the Zionist banner.

This medal is one of a series of twelve medals entitled "The Making of the Jewish State." The set depicted events culminating in the establishment of the State of Israel and, when placed together, formed a Magen David.

143. Card inscribed: 18 Herzl 10 Sheqalim Coins

Israel Government Coins and Medals Corporation
Issuer: Bank of Israel
Producer: Swiss Federal Mint
Israel, 1984
Silver
Sheet measures 8 1/4 x 5 in.

Herzl's image was used in Israel for a banknote and for these coins. Herzl's left profile is highlighted against a background which includes his name in raised lettering, repeated again and again, a form of design rarely found in coins.

144. Medal

Artist: Dora de Pedery Hunt
Obverse: THEODOR HERZL
Reverse: FIRST ZIONIST CONGRESS BASEL, 1987
Private Issue
Canada, 1987
Bronze
4 x 3 3/4 in.

The irregular shape of this medal is unusual. Its creator was inspired to produce a Herzl medal after hearing a lecture delivered by Mr. Anson.

Herzliana for the Home

A vast assortment of artifacts bearing Herzl's image have been produced in a variety of media. Although some of the artifacts bearing Herzl's image were functional, like pipe rests and sugar tongs, the majority were purely decorative. Since these items were intended for the general population, they were mass produced in inexpensive metals and woods. In Eretz Israel, the use of olivewood for tourist trade items added a local touch. Despite the imprimatur of respectability that the late 19th century Arts and Crafts movements placed on crafts, and the artistry of the works produced by the Bezalel School, most Herzl souvenirs do not aspire to a high level of craftsmanship.

Busts of famous individuals were among the bibelots with which people decorated their home, displaying their commitment to aesthetics as well as political and social causes. Busts of Herzl were created in many media. While most were purely decorative, at least one hollow version has a slot enabling it to function as a bank.

Perhaps the most familiar image of Herzl is that based on E.M. Lilien's photograph of Theodor Herzl on the balcony of the Three Kings Hotel, overlooking the Rhine. It was published in *Ost und West* #8/9 (1904), and was copied in many different forms and materials, including woven rugs.

Plaques with Herzl's image were used to decorate both interior and exterior walls of people's homes. One even bears traces of the blue paint with which the exterior of many homes were painted. Many of these souvenirs reflect the aesthetics of popular artistic forms. Some of the earlier examples of these plaques show the influence of the sinuous lines of Art Nouveau, and the Bezalel School's experiments with Hebrew lettering in modern form influenced by Islamic arabesque. The creation of the State of Israel inspired the production of many new items bearing images of Herzl, often juxtaposed with a map of Israel, an expression of the popular identification of Herzl as father of the State.

Souvenir dishes and plates with Herzl's image were produced cheaply in copper using an assembly line method. Repetition of forms and the incorporation of separate elements such as roundels depicting Herzl enabled even relatively unskilled workers to produce pieces. Frequently, areas were left blank and inscribed for presentation.

145. Plaque

Artist: R.S.H.
Copyright: L.C. Mayers(?)
Inscription: Theodor Herzl
Probably England or America, 1918
Bronze
9 x 6 1/2 in.

There are twenty five plaques depicting Herzl in this exhibition, executed in a variety of media including olive wood, bronze, and plaster. This example has a delicate Art Nouveau border.

146. Plaque

Boris Schatz (1867–1932)

Hebrew inscriptions: In memory of Herzl;
If you will it it is no dream
Eretz Israel, early 20th century
Bronze; mounted on wood
Plaque 5 1/2 x 6 1/2, wooden mount 8 x 9 1/2 in.

Boris Schatz produced several items commemorating Theodor Herzl, including paintings and medals. This is a large version of a medal which depicts Herzl juxtaposed with a figure of Moses,

equating the two heroes of the Jews who led their people to Eretz Israel but did not live to see their vision fulfilled. The lettering is executed in typical Bezalel manner, drawn from the wellsprings of Art Nouveau combined with decorative Islamic forms.

147. Plaque

Bezalel
Hebrew inscription: Herzl
Tin, mounted on wood
Jerusalem, early 20th century
6 3/4 x 5 1/4 in.

This simple plaque produced at Bezalel shows the influence of the English Arts and Crafts movement under William Morris in its use of simple materials and the exposure of connective elements such as the rivets which hold the plaque to the wooden base.

148. Plate with Damascene Decoration

Bezalel
Jerusalem, early 20th century
Bronze, copper, silver
D: 9 in.

Damascene refers to the inlay of copper and silver in brass. The name reflects the traditional association of this technique with Damascus. The Bezalel School produced many craft items, often, as with the damascene decoration of this piece, the techniques evoke local associations. Works

produced at Bezalel had a propagandistic side; they demonstrated that Jews were able to create art, and that such production was in progress in Eretz Israel under Zionist auspices.

149. Decorative cover for Memo Pad

Inscription: Dr. Herzl
Bezalel School
Jerusalem, early 20th century
Wood, embossed leather, copper plaque
8 1/4 x 6 1/4 in H: 1 1/4 in

Artisans trained at the Bezalel art school, earned their living by producing artifacts such as this which were functional yet decorative. These items were executed in what was described as a Jewish national style, illustrating the ability of Jews to be both artistic and productive craftsmen. At the same time, items decorated with images of national heroes such as Herzl demonstrated the societal and political values of both the artisan and the eventual purchaser.

150. Two Wall Hangings

Alliance Israelite Universelle School
Jerusalem, first quarter of the 20th century
42 x 24 in. each including fringe

Anton Felton recently suggested that a popular series of wall hangings depicting famous personal-

ities was produced in the Alliance Israelite Universelle School in Jerusalem early in this century. The school produced right and left profile views of Herzl leaning on a balcony looking at people who fill the valley between his vantage point and the Tower of David, a view based on Lilien's popular photograph of Herzl. A third version depicts Herzl from the front, standing with arms crossed. Other notable figures reproduced in this series include Lord Balfour and Herbert Samuel, the first high commissioner of Eretz Israel (1920–1925).

151. *Plaque for suspension*

Hebrew inscription: Joseph Trumpeldor
(1880–1920)
Lead
4 3/4 x 4 in.

Depictions of heroes of the *yishuv* (settlement) were popular during the 1930s and 1940s. Three pieces (cat. nos. 151–153) in the Anson collection appear to form all or part of a set of such heroes. These pieces are unusual; the face of the hero is inscribed in the center of a Magen David (Star of David) intertwined with a wreath. A suspension

loop suggests that these were intended to be hung on a wall rather than displayed flat in a case.

Trumpeldor was a pioneer soldier who had served in the Russian army and went on to become a Jewish national hero. He organized the defense of the Jewish settlements in the Upper Gaililee, and died in an Arab attack on Tel Hai.

152. *Plaque for suspension*

Hebrew Inscription: Dr. T. Herzl
Lead
4 3/4 x 4 in.

This plaque depicting Herzl was apparently made at the same time as those of Trumpeldor and Arlosoroff, possibly as part of a set depicting contemporary heroes.

153. *Plaque for suspension*

Hebrew inscription: Chaim Arlosoroff
(1899–1933)
Lead
4 3/4 x 4 in.

A leader of the Zionist labor movement, Arlosoroff was a member of the 1926 yishuv (settlement) delegation to the League of Nations Permanent Mandates Commission. He was assassinated in 1933 while organizing the emigration of Jews from Nazi Germany.

154. *Plate*

Inscription: "If I forget you, O Jerusalem, let my right hand wither..." Psalm 137.5
First half of 20th century
Copper; enamel
D: 11 3/4 in.

The imagery on this plate is unusual, combining a frontal image of Herzl with Zionst flags, a Magen David, and a prominent depiction of a Jewish National Fund stamp.

CAT. NO. 154

155. Spoon

Hebrew Inscription: Herzl
Silver plated brass
Mid 20th century
5 3/4 x 1 1/4 in.

Silver spoons and sugar tongs were popular gifts; many tourist venues sold and still sell spoons decorated with images of the tourist site or a famous individual connected with it. This spoon is decorated with a profile image of Herzl.

156. Bust of Herzl

Hebrew inscription: Theodor Herzl
Possibly before 1948
900 Silver
Collection of Isaac Genack z'l
7 x 5 3/4 in.

This exhibition includes nine busts depicting Theodor Herzl, executed in bronze, plaster and silver.

The use of silver for this bust makes it unusual in comparison with the multitude of examples created of plaster and bronze. Mr. Genack was an ardent Zionist, and donated the 1895 oil portrait of Herzl by G. Wertheimer to the Knesset. (illus. on p. 8)

157. Bust of Herzl

Artist: Ivan Sors (1895 – ca. 1959)
Inscription: Theodor Herzl
Reverse: If you will it is no dream
U.S.A., 1948
Plaster, unpainted
11 x 8 x 6 3/4 in.

This bust is the only effigy in the Anson collection which bears a date.

Plaster bears a slight resemblance to stone, the material traditionally used to preserve the features of rulers, heroes and the wealthy. As an inexpensive medium, busts produced in plaster were easily purchased by Zionists who wished to decorate their homes with images of national heroes. (illus. on p. 8)

158. Bookend

Artist: Ivan Sors (1895 – ca. 1959)
Inscription: If You Will It,
Is No Dream; Theodor Herzl
Copyright Israel, 1948
Metal
5 3/4 x 4 1/4 in.

There are four pairs of bookends and one single bookend in this exhibition. While most of these are flat, this example is shaped like a bust of Herzl.

159. Bookends

Hebrew inscriptions: 1897 Generations of Zionism 1947 If You Will It, It Is Not A Dream
Israel, ca. 1948
Bronze, enamel
4 x 4 3/4 x 3 1/2 in

Bookends were popular Israeli products, especially after the establishment of the State of Israel. These are shaped like an open book. Herzl's left profile is juxtaposed against the emblem of the State of Israel, a visual metaphor expressing the importance of Herzl in the context of the State. The turquoise enamel used in the decoration was very popular around the 1950s in Israel.

160. Dish

Hebrew inscription:
The State of Israel 5 Iyar 1948
Copper
D: 9 1/2 in.

Twelve plates or dishes representing the variety of types in the Anson collection were selected for exhibition. A group of these incorporate a map of Israel, the national flag, and an image of Herzl.

161. Plate

Inscriptions: IN COMMEMORATION OF THE JEWISH STATE ISRAEL 1948 The Lord's Promise to Abraham Isaac Jacob
Inscriptions on reverse: Gen. 8.15; Gen. 26.3; Gen. 28.13
Porcelain
D: 10 in.

The inscription on this plate serves to locate the authorization for the Jewish homeland in Israel to the Biblical period from which this promise in Genesis dates. The incorporation of Herzl's image reminds the viewer of the recent Zionist struggles, and the heroic figure who was credited with fathering the movement. The borders of Israel depicted on this plate are those which postdated the conflict following the withdrawl of the United Nations from Jerusalem.

162. Plate

Republic of Israel May 14. 1948
If You Will it it is No Legend
Inscription, reverse: First Edition Dedicated to the Pioneers of Palestine
Produced by Stores, Inc.
Newark, New Jersey
Porcelain; 23 Karat Gold
D: 10 5/8 in.

This souvenir plate was produced to celebrate the establishment of the State of Israel. The central motif depicts the borders of the new country. Zionist banners, now the official flag of the State, decorate the borders. While Herzl himself is not

CAT. NO. 162

portrayed on this piece, his prophetic quotation is featured prominently. There is an error in the Hebrew inscription.

The map shows the partition recommended by the United Nations Special Committee on Palestine (UNSCOP), which isolated Jerusalem as an International Zone. The dark regions on this map note the territory the committee suggested be allotted to the Jews.

163. Plate

Hebrew inscriptions: "State of Israel; Binyamin Ze'ev Herzl; If you will it it is not a dream"
Israel, ca. 1948
Copper
D: 11 3/4 in.

The folk character of this piece can be seen in the naive rendering of the portrait, and the fact that a word has been omitted in the Hebrew inscription.

164. Menorah

Inscription: The New Light for Israel
[Hebrew and English]
Ca. 1948
Brass
22 x 19 1/2 x 6 in.

Among the artifacts celebrating the existence of the State of Israel is this menorah. The text of the 1948 declaration of the State of Israel (in Hebrew and English) decorates the top of this menorah. Herzl is depicted in left profile on one face of the base, as if supervising the arrival and welcome of people to Israel. Henrietta Szold (1860–1945) and Hadassah Hospital are portrayed on the opposite face.

165. Plaque

Sculptor: Klein
Hebrew inscription: Dr. Binyamin Zeev Herzl Iyar 1860 to Tammuz 1904
Producer: Pal Bel
Ca. 1950s
Bronze
5 3/4 x 4 1/4 in.

The Pal Bel company produced a range of ritual and decorative souvenirs that are now regarded as collectors' items.

166. Plaque

Sculptor: Klein
Hebrew inscription: Dr. Herzl
Producer: Pal Bel
Israel, ca. 1950
Bronze
4 3/4 x 3 in.

CAT. NO. 164

167. Plaque

B. Afroyim (1893–1984)
Hebrew and English inscriptions:
Theodor Herzl 1860–1904
Israel, 1955
Bronze
23 x 15 3/4 in.

This plaque depicting Herzl is unusual for both its size and the comprehensiveness of its markings. The artist designed plaques depicting other distinguished Jewish figures including Golda Meir.

168. Dish

Hebrew inscription: If you will it it is not a dream
Jerusalem, Israel, ca. 1950s
Copper, enamel
D: 9 1/2 in.

This dish was executed with the patinated surface typical of its time. The central medallion is decorated with a profile image of Herzl.

169. Dish

Hebrew inscription: If you will it it is not a dream
1860–1960; Israel
Israel
Copper, enamel
D: 7 1/2 in.

The centennial of Herzl's birth, which coincided with the twelfth anniversary of the State of Israel, provided a new impetus for the production of Herzl souvenirs in Israel to commemorate the figure who loomed so large in popular imagination in connection with the foundation of the State of Israel.

Herzl as Popular Icon

Herzl's image is paramount in the secular Zionist hagiography, an icon of the Jewish nationalist movement, functioning as a link between the Jewish past and present, and between religious and non-religious Jew. Handsome and charismatic, a lawyer and journalist, he personified the acculturated European sophisticate, a manly, respectable bourgeois, the antithesis of the stereotypic *shtetl* Jew. Herzl's luxurious beard suggested both traditional images of prophets and the beard of traditional Judaism.

Many artists were motivated to depict Herzl, drawn by his handsome appearance as well as his socio-political importance. Hermann Struck (1876–1944) created several impressive etchings of Herzl. He referred to Herzl in a memorial album as a man of impressive superhuman beauty, an ideal type, possessing a kingliness of mien and bearing.

The artist E.M. Lilien (1874–1925), a delegate to the Fifth Congress in Basel, created the oft-copied 1901 photograph of Herzl on the balcony of Zurich's Three Kings hotel. Frequently, this pose was combined with traditional images of holy sites such as the Western Wall and David's Tower which made the historical landscape of Eretz Israel part of the Zionist experience and evoked the shared history of world Jewry. After Herzl's death, this image became increasingly popular due to the evocative connotations of this motif which seems to portray Herzl gazing into the future in Eretz Israel. It was combined with newer popular Zionist images such as the rising sun, symbol of Zionist hopes; and images of pioneers rebuilding the land of Israel. Other works by Lilien popularized Herzl's image for Biblical figures, and for the face of an angel in his 1902 illustrations for *Lieder des Ghetto*.

Postcards were a popular new method of communication in the late nineteenth century; in addition to being used to exchange greetings, they were avidly collected in albums. Images of Herzl were used on postcards time and again, varied only by the presence or absence of inscriptions. The majority of these images of Herzl show his left profile.

Material culture served to disseminate Herzl's image, drawing on Herzl's importance as a Zionist icon, but not always for a Zionist purpose; his features were adopted by other organizations both in Israel and abroad, and occasionally by commercial firms with no political agenda. For those who purchased souvenirs depicting Herzl, or received an item decorated with his image in return for a contribution, the images provided access to Zionism past and present, and imparted a sense of participation in its continuity and success.

170. Postcard: Dr. Theodor Herzl

Inscription dated Kiev February 2, 1901
Published by Verlag Isidor Knopf
Vienna
3 1/2 x 5 1/2 in.

This appears to be an early example of the commercial use of Herzl's image not produced for Zionist purposes. Herzl's left profile is inscribed in a cartouche above a Magen David (Star of David) within which is a rampant lion. The cartouche is framed with floral motifs, and owes its appearance to the decorative vocabulary of traditional sentimental Victorian forms. The sender's inscription mentions the Easter holidays.

171. Postcard: Dr. Herzl
(Russian and Hebrew)

Hebrew inscription: Zion
Lithographer/artist: E. I. Marcus
St. Petersburg, Russia 1903
5 1/2 x 3 3/4 in.

Given the fact that relatively few Herzl postcards can be attributed to a specific publisher, it is interesting that this example, printed in Tsarist Russia, is both signed and dated.

172. Micrographic portrait

ALT NEU LAND
DR THEODOR HERZL
Print
24 x 10 in.

Micrography is a traditional Jewish art form dating back to approximately the eleventh century. Decorative forms are produced using the words of a text, written with very tiny letters. The words can either outline shapes, as you see here in the crossed branches, or can be used to fill in a shape as has been done with Herzl's hair and beard. A text from Herzl's *Altneuland*, published in 1902, has been used to compose a portrait of the author.

CAT. NO. 170

173. New Year's Postcard

FEDERATIA SIONISTA IN ROMANIA
(Zionist Federation of Romania)
Tip. Fränkel
1903
Postmark FOCBAN 10 Sep 1904
3 3/4 x 5 1/2 in.

This Zionist New Year's greeting with an image of Herzl was produced for 1903, but used in 1904 after Herzl's death. Pasted near the image of Herzl is a JNF stamp inscribed Zion in Hebrew. It was the most popular JNF stamp sold between 1902 and 1914.

174. Postcard: Dr. Theodor Herzl on the Bridge over the Rhine in Basel

Photographer: E.M. Lilien (1874–1925)
Inscribed by William H. Hechler (1845–1931)
Verlag "Zion"
Vienna, 1904
5 1/2 x 3 1/2 in.

The photograph on which this postcard is based was taken by Lilien in Basel in 1901. Herzl, shown in left profile, leans on the railing of the balcony of the Three Kings Hotel, the Rhine river in the background. One of the most popular images of Herzl, this pose was adapted for use on stamps, textiles, and postcards. Often scenes of sites in Eretz Israel were combined with this image.

William Henry Hechler (1835–1831) served as tutor to the children of Friederich, Grand Duke of Baden, uncle of Kaiser Wilhelm II. Hechler worked to establish a relationship between Herzl, the Grand Duke, and the Kaiser, and accompanied Herzl in 1898 when he went to Eretz Israel to meet Kaiser Wilhelm. (illus. on p. 26)

CAT. NO. 175

175. Postcard: Die Erschaffung des Menschen (The Creation of Man)

Artist: E. M. Lilien (1874–1925)
From Rosenfeld's *Lieder des Ghetto* (Songs of the Ghetto)
Verlag B. Harz
Berlin N. 24
3 3/4 x 5 1/2

Lilien, a Jew from a traditional background in Eastern Europe, illustrated the poetic anthology, *Lieder des Ghetto* in 1902. These illustrations were often reproduced in Zionist materials. His style is based on the German form of Art Nouveau known as *Jugendstil*. In this image, Lilien depicted Herzl as an angel. While many viewers are surprised that Lilien chose to depict Herzl in the nude, it was a standard motif of German nationalist movements, where heroic male figures are depicted nude in a classicizing manner. This served Zionist purposes as well, underlining the vigor of this Zionist leader and the similarity between the Jewish nationalist movement and other contemporary nationalist movements.

176. Postcard Depicting Herzl

Hebrew inscription: Herzl born 10 Iyar 1860 2 May 1860 died 20 Tammuz 1904 4 July 1904
Postmark Russia, 1905
5 3/4 x 3 3/4 in.

Most images of Herzl show his left profile, as does this one.

177. Postcard: Portrait of Herzl

Hebrew inscription: Herzl's vision
Keren Kayemet le-Israel
1905
5 1/2 x 3 1/2 in.

The inscription on this reproduction of the JNF Herzl stamp makes the message very clear: Herzl's dream was to see Eretz Israel become a refuge for exiled Jews of Russia and Poland.

178. Watch With Face Depicting Herzl

Brass; gold plate, glass, paper
Early 20th century
2 1/2 x 1 3/4 in.

Paper watch dials could be purchased depicting Herzl full face so that individuals might customize their pocket watch. The primary numbers on these faces are Hebrew rather than Arabic, although the numbers for the second hand are Arabic. The use of Hebrew lettering here reminds us of the Zionist goal for Hebrew to be the official language of the movement and the country.

CAT. NO. 178

179. Postcard: Jerusalem: Die Davidsburg.

(Jerusalem City of David)
H.L.i.W. – Ph. 6
Kunstlerkarte 272, Ser. Z.2.
Eretz Israel, 1911
Postmark: Festyn Zyd. z. Czerwca 1912
5 1/2 x 3 1/2 in.

Set into an upper corner of a photographic image of the Tower of David is a depiction of the JNF Herzl stamp which shows Herzl and the Tower. Such imagery reminded Zionists of both the historical past of the Jews in Eretz Israel, and present efforts to make the land a refuge for the Jewish people.

180. Paper Square

Hebrew inscription: Born 10 Iyar 1860 died 20 Tammuz 1904
Geprüft u. freigegeben Pressev.
Lit. Golubczyk
Warschau 15/6 1917
5 1/2 x 3 3/4 in.

This piece is decorated with a selection of Zionist motifs. Herzl's left profile framed in a Magen David (Star of David) is set against an idealistic landscape of Eretz Israel.

181. Sheet Music: Hatikvoh (The Hope),
The Jewish National Anthem

Words and music by L.M. Imber
Arranged by I.J. Kammen
Published by J. & J. Kammen
Brooklyn, New York, 1919
14 x 10 5/8 in.

Like other contemporary nationalist organizations, Zionism had its own heroes, symbols, and songs. The cover of this Hatikvah song sheet depicts the primary Zionist hero, Herzl, flanked by two Zionist banners. The Magen David (Star of David) on these banners resembles the popular JNF Zion stamp.

CAT. NO. 182

182. Portrait of Herzl

Hebrew inscription: Dr. T. Herzl
Atlas Weaving Factory
Tel-Aviv, 1920s
Silk; machine woven; cardboard mount
Central section 13 3/4 x 8 1/2 in.
Open 13 3/4 x 19 in.

This woven portrait of Herzl produced by the Atlas Weaving Factory was commonly removed from its cardboard mount, framed, and hung on the wall. A postcard in the Anson collection reproduces this image.

183. Portrait of Herzl

Y. Ben Dor
Hebrew inscription on mat:
"Within fifty years, the State of Israel willl be an established fact—Herzl"
Handwritten Hebrew inscription: "Herzl Room, Stern House, 83 Memeila Street, Jerusalem"
Bezalel
Jerusalem, early 20th century
Photograph
9 1/4 x 6 3/4 in.

This unusual portrait of Herzl was taken from slightly behind him, although it shows his famous

left profile. The photograph was probably taken during the year before his death. The masterful handling of the medium is more artistic than the usual photographs of Herzl taken for documentary purposes.

184. Sheet Music: Hatikwoh; Jewish National Anthem (Russian and English)

Published by Lieberman's Publishing House
Music Publisher: Free Song
Odessa, early 20th century
10 x 6 3/4 in.

The covers of many early examples of sheet music for Hatikvah such as this one were decorated with an image of Herzl, either alone or in the company of other prominent Zionist figures.

185. Postcard: Zum 25. Todestag DR. THEODOR HERZL (On the 25th Anniversary of the Death of Dr. Theodor Herzl)

Postmark VII.29.12
5 3/4 x 4 1/4 in

Significant anniversaries of the birth and death of Herzl were the occasion for production of new postcards. Aside from official Zionist products by organizations such as JNF, the Jüdischer Verlag, Libanon and Phoenix, publishers often did not bother to sign their work, and it is reasonable to assume that these unknowns were motivated more by profit than other concerns.

186. Printing Plate for Zion Album Song Sheet

Early 20th century
Copper and wood
12 3/4 x 9 1/4 x 1 in.

Among the unusual items in the Anson collection is this printing plate, used to produce sheet music. In fact, the Zion Album song sheet (cat. no. 187) was printed from this plate.

187. Sheet Music: ZION ALBUM HATIKVOH UND DORT WU DIE ZEDER

Arranged by Henry Russotto
Cover designed by Louis Terr
Hebrew Publishing Co.
New York, early 20th century
12 1/4 x 9 1/4

Zionists solidified their sense of community by singing nationalist songs, the most popular of which was Hatikvah (The Hope), expressing longing for Eretz Israel. Portraits of Herzl and Nordau adorn this cover, which is ironic in view of the fact that the two gentlemen did not approve of the character of the composer Naphtali Herz Imber (1856–1909), an alcoholic, rumored to have converted to Christianity.

188. Postcard Depicting Herzl

Artist: A.G
Hebrew incription:
If You Will It It Is Not A Dream
Goldbergs Press
Postmark 1934
3 3/4 x 5 3/4 in.

The artist's emphasis on development and technology, the buildings and factories of a modern city, the railroad line and the ship speeding towards Eretz Israel, suggest that the Herzl quotation here refers to the achievements of the Jewish people in Eretz Israel. A right profile image of Herzl is depicted on the left.

189. New Year's Postcard

Artist: Yitzhak Gafni
Hebrew inscription: A good year
Jerusalem, first half of the 20th century
3 3/4 x 5 3/4

This card, representative of a type popular during the early 20th century, places the Lilien photograph of Herzl in Basel at the center of traditional sites in Eretz Israel. Images such as this made the landscape familiar to many Zionists, even those who did not visit the land itself. At the same time, it reminded Zionists of the shared history of the Jewish people and that, in common with other nationalist movements, Jews possessed a national homeland.

CAT. NO. 189

190. Postcard Depicting Herzl

Inscription: Theodor Herzl 2nd May 1860 – 3rd July 1904 (Hebrew and English)
England, great England, whose gaze sweeps over all the seas—free England—will understand and sympathize with the aims and aspirations of Zionism. (Theodor Herzl at the 4th Zionist Congress, London 1900).
Inscription date 1944
5 1/2 x 3 1/2 in.

The quotation from Herzl's speech at the Zionist Congress accompanies a depiction of his left profile.

191. Postcard Depicting Herzl

Hebrew inscription: Dr. Benjamin Zeev Herzl
Alt-Neuland
Artist: Prof. Perec Willenberg
Poland, 1946
5 3/4 x 4 in.

The artist presents us with a traditional image incorporating artifacts relating to the life of the individual commemorated. A portrait of Herzl tops an altar-like form on which are books and other artifacts relating to Herzl's literary and Zionist careers.

192. Hebrew New Year's Card

Blessings for a new year
Israel, 1948
2 1/4 x 4 1/4 in.

Moses and Herzl, the visionaries who guided their people to Eretz Israel but did not live to see the culmination of their vision, flank an Israeli city on this New Year's card dating from the time of the birth of the new State. This image both confirms Herzl's status, and places him in the context of Jewish history and heroes.

193. Postcard with Poem "Land! Land!"

Artist: Lola
Poem by M. Raskin
5 1/2 x 3 3/4 in.

This appears to be an early image incorporating the figure of Herzl after his death, indicating that he is still guiding exiled Jews to the Promised Land.

CAT. NO. 194

194. Handkerchief with New Year's greetings in Yiddish

Possibly mid-20th century
Cotton; printed
10 x 10 in.

Handkerchiefs and scarves decorated with images of popular figures were increasingly popular during this period.

195. Portrait of Theodor Herzl

Artist: Saul Raskin (1878–1966)
Inscribed: Binyamin Zeev Herzl [Hebrew]
Dr. Theodore [sic] Herzl
New York, 20th century
Engraving
15 1/4 x 11 in.

Raskin, a painter and engraver, was known for his scenes of Jewish life in New York and Eretz Israel. Unlike Struck, Schatz and Lilien, Raskin never

met Herzl, and this profile portrait was probably based on either Struck's famous version, or a photograph.

196. Postcard Depicting Herzl

Hebrew inscription: Binyamin Zeev Herzl
Keren Kayemet le-Israel
Israel, postmark Day of Issue, Haifa 1954
5 1/4 x 3 1/2 in.

197. Paper Rectangle

Hebrew inscription: If You Will It It Is Not
A Dream 10 Iyar 1860–20 Tammuz 1904
1860–1960
Golubczyk
Warszawa
3 1/4 x 5 1/2 in.

This piece was produced for the anniversary of Herzl's birth. Selected Zionist symbols include Herzl's left profile framed by a Magen David (Star of David), juxtaposed against a seven-branched menorah.

198. Postcard: Kopie der offiziellen Postkarte XV Zionistenkongress, Basel 1927 (Copy of the official postcard of the XV Zionist Congress, Basel 1927)

Postmark Tel Aviv 31.8.60 and Basel 31.8.60
5 3/4 x 3 3/4 in.

199. Theodor Herzl

Artist: Hermann Struck (1876–1944)
Jüdischer Verlag
Berlin, 20th century
Framed: 28 3/4 x 24 3/4 in.

In this image, Herzl stands with his hands resting on the back of a chair. This depiction is encountered less frequently than Struck's left profile image of Herzl (cat. no. 201).

CAT. NO. 199

200. Portrait of Herzl after painting by J. Koppay

Jerusalem, 1960
16 1/4 x 13 in.

The original of this portrait of Herzl was executed by J. Koppay in 1903. This print after the portrait was issued by the Joint Committee of the Government and the Zionist Organization Executive in commemoration of the 100th anniversary of Herzl's birth, underlining the continuing importance of Herzl's image in the self identification of the government of Israel and the Zionist organization. (also illus on p. 16)

201. Herzl Prophet and Creator of the State of Israel

Artist: Hermann Struck (1876–1944)
Publisher: Shikmona
Impression Orell Füssli Sig. Zürich
Haifa, Israel, 1961
Engraving
Collection of Stanley I. Batkin
27 3/4 x 11 1/2 in. framed

This is one of the popular images of Herzl produced by artist Hermann Struck, who met Herzl in Vienna in 1903.

202. Postcard Depicting Herzl

Inscription: THEODOR HERZL
9225
Palphot Ltd.
Herzlia, Israel, postmark 1.1.86
5 3/4 x 4 in.

Lilien's photograph of Herzl leaning on the railing of the balcony of the Dreie Könige Hotel in Basel is reproduced on both this postcard and the stamp.

203. Postcard Depicting Herzl

Hebrew inscription: "If I forget you, O Jerusalem, let my right hand wither." (Psalms 137.5)
Israel, 1986
5 1/2 x 3 1/2 in.

Reproductions of the image used on the JNF stamp depicting Herzl leaning on the railing of the hotel balcony overseeing the entry of refugees to Jerusalem, opposite the Tower of David were exceedingly popular postcard motifs.

CAT. NO. 201

Herzl in Our Time

The power of Herzl's image endures. It symbolizes the achievements of the Jewish people, the strength of the world Jewish community, and the restoration to Jewish hands of the Jewish homeland, the State of Israel. Plays dealing with Herzl's life have been produced in New York City, Toronto and Israel. The Zionist Congresses, lectures and symposia continue to be held, generating additional memorabilia. In 1960, Herzl's *Old New Land* was reprinted, illustrated with scenes of contemporary Israel and its recent history. Copies of Herzl's diaries and other works, new biographies, and reprints of old biographies continually appear. Travel brochures to attract the Jewish customer tout the presence in their cities of sites related to Herzl's life.

The centennial of the First Zionist Congress in 1997 has spawned a profusion of commercial items decorated with Zionist imagery, including Herzl. Among these items are color reproductions of postcards depicting Herzl and his family, as well as T-shirts and other typical souvenir items of our time. Such artifacts of popular culture demonstrate a continuing cultural investment in the Herzl legend and its objectives, and continue to govern its expression and the common perception of its manifestations. It is also apparent that the concept of Jewish nationalism, linked to the Land of Israel but which neither requires residence in the Land, nor excludes patriotism towards one's country of residence, has succeeded. Despite the recent trend which questions the cost of Jewish nationalism, it remains a powerful force. And individuals the world over continue to purchase articles depicting Herzl as a way of identifying with Jewish nationalism, and demonstrating support for Israel.

---

204. *Grand vin rouge d'Israel*

Reserve du jubilee Dr. Theodor Herzl
Ben Ami, No. 9312
Marcel Hess M.C.F.A.
Dist. Cave Arnold Bocklin Bale
Askalon Wines–Carmei Zion Ltd.
Israel, 1983
H: 1 foot; D: 3 in.

The consumption and connoisseurship of wine has enjoyed a growth in popularity across a broad spectrum of the population during the last quarter of the twentieth century. Kosher wines, many produced from grapes grown in Israel, have now became available in relative profusion, ranging from mixtures of grapes such as this red wine to Zinfandels and Merlots.

The balcony image of Herzl at the Three Kings Hotel, on the label of this bottle, reminds the viewer how far Jews have come since Herzl stood there. Israel is a reality, not a dream, and among the items it produces is this wine! The consumer is subliminally called upon to purchase this wine in order to participate in the Zionist achievement.

205. *Bag of Chocolate Coins with Portrait of Herzl*

Hebrew inscription obverse: Binyamin Zeev Herzl
Hebrew inscription reverse: Israel – Elite – Israel
Plastic, metal foil, chocolate
Late 20th century
5 x 2 in.

These chocolate coins are decorated with a right profile image of Theodor Herzl. Chocolate coins are popular holiday treats especially on Hanukkah when they resemble "Hanukkah gelt." This use of Herzl's image bridges the past and present, the historical Maccabees, heroes of Hanukkah, and Herzl, the hero of Zionism in our own time.

CAT. NO. 208

206. *Shopping bag*

Hebrew inscription: The First Hundred Years of Zionism
The World Zionist Organization
Israel, 1996
19 1/2 x 12 in

The imagery on this shopping bag is quite simple, consisting of the text itself and an image of Herzl, in blue on the white bag, recalling the traditional Zionist colors and the flag of the State of Israel.

207. *Herzl T-shirt*

Club Sportswear
Studio David Harel Ltd.
Jerusalem, 1996
Package 14 1/2 x 12 in.

Modern heroes including Albert Einstein have been memorialized on T-shirts, so it should come as no surprise that there is a T shirt with a traditional image of Herzl, colored to suit contemporary taste. Considering Herzl's sense of sartorial propriety, the use of his image as decoration for a garment which developed from underclothing makes a statement about contemporary culture.

208. *Telephone card attached to letter from Dr. Federbush*

Bezeq
Israel, 1996
2 1/4 x 3 1/2 in.
Mount: 8 3/8 x 5 3/8 in.

One of the more recent conjunctions of technolo-gy and contemporary popular culture is this pre-paid telephone card. A silhouette of Herzl's left profile, the quotation "If you will it it is no dream," and a Magen David inscribed with a rampant lion are juxtaposed against a bustling Israeli street scene.

209. *Pamphlet*

100 Years of Zionism
Israel Postal Authority
Philatelic Service
Israel, 1996
19 1/4 x 27 1/4 in.

The Israel Postal Authority took advantage of the Zionist centennial to celebrate its own history with the publication of a poster and pamphlets illustrating stamps it had produced with Zionist themes. These included four stamps with images of Herzl.

210. *Folder with Postcards:*

100 years of Zionism
Israel, 1996
Folder: 4 1/2 x 6 1/2 in.

A group of traditional postcard images of Herzl and his family were recolored and produced in this format for the centennial of the First Zionist Congress. This image, included in the package, is taken from a poster, an example of which is also in the exhibition (cat. no. 215). Herzl's left profile is placed against a background of 92 faces, including those of Sir Moses Montefiore, Rabbi Abraham Isaac Kook, and Golda Meir. The style and color owe much to the work of Andy Warhol.

211. *Travel Brochure for Jewish Basel*

Swissair
ca. 1990s
8 3/4 x 4 1/4 in.

This recent travel brochure directed at the Jewish market promotes Basel as the home of the Zionist Congress.

212. Street Sign

Herzl Street
Brooklyn, New York
Metal, enamel
9 x 24 in.

An original street sign, this piece was found among a collection of street signs which had been replaced by New York City officials in favor of new designs.

213. Street Sign

Rehov Herzl
Hebrew inscription: Rehov Binyamin Zeev
Theodor Herzl 2.5.1860 – 3.7.1904
Tel-Aviv
8 1/2 x 19 in

This is a reproduction of the Tel-Aviv street sign, specially commissioned for the Anson collection.

Posters

The poster has been a popular art form of the last century. Herzl's image is well represented during the period covered by this section of the exhibition. Centennials and Congresses have provided the primary impetus for the creation of these contemporary posters, although JNF fundraising efforts are also represented.

214. Poster

The Children's Forest in the Mountains of Jerusalem
Association of Teachers on behalf of the Keren Kayemet le-Israel
The year of Herzl 5720
Calendar of Gifts
Jewish National Fund
1960
20 1/2 x 28 in.

215. Poster

Hebrew inscription: Herzl Year
One hundred years since the First Zionist Congress
World Zionist Organization
Ministry of Education, Culture and Sport
Israel, 1960
37 3/4 x 26 1/4 in.

216. Poster

40th Anniversary of the State
Hebrew inscription: In the year 1897 the First Zionist Congress convened under the herald of the visionary Theodor Herzl calling on the people to establish a national homeland in its land
State Office of Education and Culture
Israel, 1987
36 x 24 1/4 in.

217. Poster

31st Zionist Congress (Hebrew and English)
Jerusalem, December 6–10, 1987
36 x 24 in. framed

218. Poster

Bank Leumi 1902–1992 from Vision to Reality 90 Years of Nation Building
39 x 27 in.

219. Poster

THEODOR HERZL SYMPOSION, WIEN, 100 JAHRE "DER JUDENSTAAT"
17–21 MARZ '96
WIENER RATHAUS [Theodor Herzl Symposium: 100 Years of The Jewish State]
Vienna, 1996
23 1/4 x 16 1/2 in.

220. Poster

Centennial of the Zionist Movement; 33rd Zionist Congress; Basel 1897–Jerusalem 1997
World Zionist Organization
11 3/4 x 8 1/4 in.

221. Poster

Hebrew inscription: Centennial of the Zionist
Movement
33rd Zionist Congress Basel 1897 – Jerusalem
1997
World Zionist Organization
36 x 24 1/4 in.

Herzl in the Theater

222. Playbill: Herzl

Palace Theatre
New York City
November 1976
Attached: tickets for Row A seats 106, 107
and 108
9 x 5 5/8 in.

223. Theater Program: Dori: A New Musical

Book and lyrics by Eric Blau
Music by Elliot Weiss
Toronto, Leah Posluns Theatre
Oct. 17 – November 9, 1984
11 x 8 3/4 in.

*224. Folder Containing Material Relating to
the Musical DORI including: a program, tickets, a poster, a press release and reviews*

Leah Posluns Theatre
Toronto, 1985
12 x 8 7/8 in.

*225. Habima Theater Program: King of
the Jews*

Written by Dvorah Omer
Music by Rami Klinstein
First Show December 19, 1992
Rovino Auditorium
9 1/2 x 7 3/4 in.

Magazines and Newspapers

The Anson collection contains numerous clippings
dealing with Herzl, but the exhibition limited the
selection of items to complete articles still in the
original publication, and to publications which feature Herzl on the cover. Among the articles in the
exhibition was one written by the collector himself for the North Jersey Jewish Standard.

Usually, articles dealing with Herzl or Zionist
subjects reproduce images from the Herzl canon.
However, artist Avi Katz paid tribute to E.M. Lilien
by adapting the latter's image of Herzl on the hotel
balcony. To update the image, Katz placed a cell
phone in Herzl's hand and substituted a modern
Israeli city for Basel.

226. Israel My Glory

"Herzl's Zionist Dream"
June/July 1996 Vol.54 No.3
11 x 8 1/2 in

227. North Jersey Jewish Standard

"Der Judenstaat": A small book with a large
vision is 100 years old"
Written by Manfred Anson
Feb. 16, 1996 Vol. LXVI No.13
14 x 10 3/4 in

228. Israel-Al

Spring 1988
13 x 10 1/2 in.

229. The Jerusalem Report

"Israel at 48: If You Can Afford It, It Is No Dream"
Volume VI No.26
May 2, 1996
Cover art by Avi Katz
10 5/8 x 8 1/4 in.

Selected Index